Glass Bead

WORKSHOP

Building Skills, Exploring Techniques, Finding Inspiration

Jeri L. Warhaftig

LARK BOOKS

A Division of Sterling Publishing Co., Inc.
New York / London

SENIOR EDITOR Valerie Van Arsdale Shrader

TECHNICAL EDITOR Chris Rich

ART DIRECTOR Kristi Pfeffer

COVER DESIGNER Cindy LaBreacht

ILLUSTRATOR Orrin Lundgren

HANDS-ON PHOTOGRAPHER Steve Mann

PROJECT PHOTOGRAPHER Stewart O'Shields

This book is dedicated to my mother, Lorry, who encourages my passions and is the mother everyone else wishes they could have, and to my extraordinary husband, Neil Fabricant, whose love, generous spirit, and ability to take on new challenges fearlessly are my inspirations.

Library of Congress Cataloging-in-Publication Data

Warhaftig, Jeri L.
  Glass bead workshop : building skills, exploring techniques, finding inspiration / Jeri L. Warhaftig. -- 1st ed.
    p. cm.
  Includes index.
  ISBN-13: 978-1-60059-123-5 (hc-plc with jacket : alk. paper)
  ISBN-10: 1-60059-123-X (hc-plc with jacket : alk. paper)
  1. Beadwork. 2. Beads. I. Title.
  TT860.W333 2008
  745.58'2--dc22

                    2007031079

10 9 8 7 6 5 4 3 2 1

First Edition

Published by Lark Books, A Division of
Sterling Publishing Co., Inc.
387 Park Avenue South, New York, NY 10016

Text © 2008, Jeri L. Warhaftig
Photography © 2008, Lark Books unless otherwise specified
Illustrations © 2008, Lark Books unless otherwise specified

Distributed in Canada by Sterling Publishing,
c/o Canadian Manda Group, 165 Dufferin Street
Toronto, Ontario, Canada M6K 3H6

Distributed in the United Kingdom by GMC Distribution Services,
Castle Place, 166 High Street, Lewes, East Sussex, England BN7 1XU

Distributed in Australia by Capricorn Link (Australia) Pty Ltd.,
P.O. Box 704, Windsor, NSW 2756 Australia

If you have questions or comments about this book, please contact:
Lark Books
67 Broadway
Asheville, NC 28801
828-253-0467

Manufactured in China

ISBN 13: 978-1-60059-123-5
ISBN 10: 1-60059-123-X

For information about custom editions, special sales, premium and corporate purchases, please contact Sterling Special Sales Department at 800-805-5489 or specialsales@sterlingpub.com.

Contents

Welcome to My Studio

Welcome to my studio and to my series of workshops in intermediate glass beadmaking. I hope that you've found your way here through your own appreciation of glass beads. Whether you're a student, collector, beadmaker, or merely a curious newcomer to this emerging and vibrant art form, you're in the right place.

Although glass has been used as an adornment for millennia, only for the last two decades or so—thanks to advancements in tools and technology—have beadmakers been able to make glass beads in modest studio settings. Classes are taught everywhere, from large commercial venues to small glass studios, so many people have tried their hands at forming glass beads in torches. But what do you do after you've learned the basics of glass bead-making? The answer to that question is the purpose of this book. Through the workshop sessions in it, I'll teach you skills and techniques that are new and different from the ones you've tried before; I'll show you materials that have emerged on the beadmaking scene during recent years; and I'll push and shove and cajole you toward finding your own creative voice and identity as a beadmaker. Let's start right now.

Who Am I?

I am a beadmaker, teacher, and passionate collector of glass beads. In the 1980s, my interest in Venetian trade beads led me to bead shows and to handmade artists' beads. After taking classes for a few years and going through the frustrations that beginners typically experience, I began my true beadmaking journey. Since then, I've had the good fortune to study with several notable bead teachers.

Together with my husband, Neil Fabricant, whom beadmakers know as "Dr. Fab," I've taught beadmaking students all over the United States and in Israel. For several years, I've been a part of the instructors' seminar offered by the International Society of Glass Beadmakers (www.isgb.org). My primary teaching focus is to help beginners turn into full-fledged beadmakers by developing my students' creative impulses so their beads will evolve in new and exciting directions.

My workshops focus on beadmaking technique—a concept that encompasses all the building blocks used to create a finished bead. What are these building blocks? They're the artist's skillful use of tools (torches, marvers, picks, presses—and more); the use of various materials (glass rods, frit, metals, and liquids); and the wide variety of methods that go into making each and every bead. They also include the beadmaker's ingenuity, tenacity, and skill, and the teacher's wisdom and patience. These building blocks can be assembled to create finished beads that reveal a wide variety of artistic expressions and techniques. The way in which each beadmaker assembles them demonstrates his or her unique creative process—and creative voice.

My own beadmaking has focused on pushing the limits of glass through alterations such as sandblasting, etching, and grinding; and the use of glass in combination with other materials, such as enamels and metals. Some of my beads are returned to the torch after annealing, then heated, reworked, and cooled all over again. Through continuous exploration of my personal relationship with glass, I've searched for my own creative voice.

Who Are You?

In this workshop, you're the student—a beadmaker seeking inspiration and an expansion of your knowledge and skills. The workshop sessions presented in this book are based on the assumption that you've mastered beginner's skills, such as heat control and the creation of symmetrical beads, but don't worry: If you're rusty or you've just plain avoided certain techniques, I offer some pointers and advice along the way that will help you tune up your techniques.

If you're already an intermediate beadmaker, you may be familiar with the materials, tools, and techniques that I teach in these sessions. For you, the value of this book

will be in the creative stretching that's included as part of every one—the section titled Further Explorations. This section will help you ask yourself, "How can I reinterpret these beads and designs to make them my own? How can I use the techniques, tools, and materials presented here to grow my own body of work?"

Guess what: Learning new things can be frustrating and hard. That was my own first experience with beadmaking. The beads that I envisioned in my head just didn't want to come out through my fingers. Over time, however, I returned to the teachings of my youth. My mother, an artist in her own right, believes that an essential part of child rearing is a daily art project. Virtually every one of my childhood days was highlighted by a time to play with our family's stock of art supplies. On different occasions, as the whim struck us, my sisters and I painted, threw clay, enameled copper, made collages, sewed doll clothes, and strung beads.

My mother knew that artistry and creativity are skills as well as talents, and that competency is born of familiarity and practice, practice, practice. Artistic skills and creativity can become instinctive, but that doesn't happen the very first time you try something new. Be patient with yourself. Attempt new skills but don't burden yourself with high expectations. Instead, take time to play, be open-minded about the creative process, sit back and watch yourself learn, and then pay attention to and appreciate your creative results. Above all, have fun.

The Basics

Although *Glass Bead Workshop* is designed for artists who have already started their love affair with glass beadmaking, the goal of this section is to get everyone, including beginners, on more or less the same page. First, I'll describe some of the essential tools and processes that you'll use. Then I'll address setting up an efficient studio and working in it safely. Finally, I'll walk you through the process of how to use this book.

Tools and Materials

Beadmakers work with a variety of tools and materials; beautiful results can be had from them all. Here we'll touch briefly on the basics of a functional glass beadmaking setup and discuss why some equipment and materials are preferable to others for certain tasks.

BASIC TOOLS

Some of the bead projects in this book require the use of specialized tools and materials; I've described these within each session and in Appendices A and B (pages 126–136). You'll also find in each session a list of the common tools—and glass—you'll need to make the main bead featured in it. Not listed, however, are a few items that many of the beads require and that every beadmaker should own. In addition to a torch and bead release, which I discuss further in the next few pages, make sure you have the following items on hand.

A small kitchen or *paring knife* is very handy. My favorite tool is a small paring knife purchased at a discount store. It has held up through years of use, but because it's so important to me, I buy more whenever I see them.

You'll also need a *³⁄₃₂-inch (2.4 mm) mandrel, a pair of rod nippers,* and a *handheld graphite or brass marver.* My *benchtop marver* is rectangular and about 1½ by 2½ inches (3.8 by 6.4 cm). I use a torch-mounted *graphite marver* as well, on which I pre-warm many bead components and steady my wrist as I work, but don't rush out to buy one. A benchtop marver will work just fine.

Of course, I own and use many (many, many, many) not-so-basic tools. It seems to me that almost all the beadmakers I meet are tool addicts—and I'm not in a position to criticize them. In this book, you'll meet some tools you may already own but perhaps aren't using, as well as tools that you may not have had a chance to try yet.

TORCHES

The workshop beads in this book were all created with a *dual-fuel, surface-mix torch* fueled by tanked oxygen and propane. Now let's review what the heck that all means.

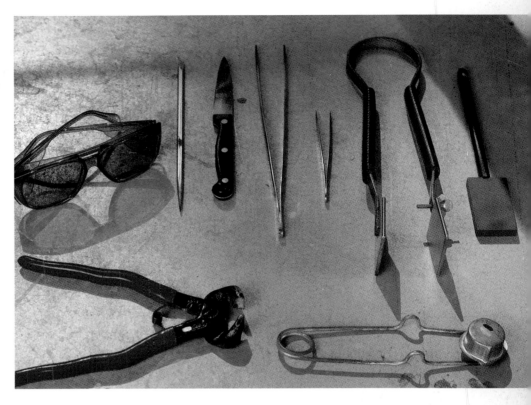

An assortment of standard tools that most beadmakers have on hand

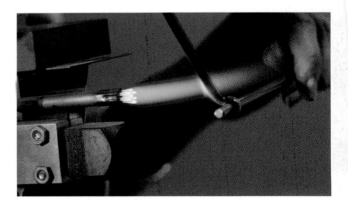

Forming a bead at the torch

The term "dual-fuel" is a bit of a misnomer, since only one gas (either propane or natural gas) really serves as a fuel. The other gas, oxygen, is an accelerant. These types of torches are sometimes referred to as "dual-gas," which is probably a more accurate term. Most beadmakers use dual-fuel torches, but many use torches that operate with canisters of a single type of gas. The practical limitation of a *single-fuel torch* is its inability to fine-tune the flame;

some of the workshop beads in this book would be difficult to make with one.

A *surface-mix torch* is one in which the fuel and oxygen are combined on the outer surface of the torch head. *Internal-mix torches*, on the other hand, combine the fuels before they exit the torch. Although there are some differences in how these two kinds of torches are operated, either type will work for the beads we'll be making.

Oxygen—the accelerant—is available in several different delivery systems; all work well for making beads. My setup usually includes tanked oxygen from a welding-supply company. I work with two tanks that are connected to each other in series and then to a regulator, which I keep set at around 12 to 14 psi (83 to 97 kPa), but your own setting will depend on the torch you're using. This setup is a real timesaver: I use the first tank until it's empty; then I close the valve on it and open the valve on the second tank. On occasion, when both tanks are empty, I switch to an *oxygen concentrator*—a medical unit intended for use by patients who need a continuous supply of oxygen. This small unit doesn't require a regulator. Its oxygen—unlike oxygen in a tank—is delivered under very low pressure; your torch will use all the oxygen it can supply. Larger concentrators are accorded the label "oxygen generators"; some of them make so much oxygen that they're used in conjunction with holding tanks that store the oxygen under pressure—just like the tanks that a gas supplier can deliver to you.

Assorted glass rods, twisties, and stringers

Dual-fuel torches are fueled by either propane or natural gas. I prefer propane, but the nice thing about natural gas is that it's already delivered to many homes, so a plumber can tap into an existing gas line, and gas will always be available to you. The disadvantage of natural gas is that residential pressure can sometimes be quite low. Devices to step up the pressure are available, but they're pricey. Natural gas, which burns with a very clean flame, seems to burn a little cooler than propane, although different torches will give different results. For my setup, I purchase propane in tanks that have roughly double the capacity of barbecue-size tanks. My propane regulator is set at about 6 psi (41 kPa).

GLASS

The beads in this book were made primarily with *Italian soft glass* (also called "soda-lime glass"), with a *coefficient of expansion* (or COE) of 104. The general rule is that all of the glass you combine in a single bead should have the same COE; glasses with different COEs aren't compatible with one another. Of course, as with any rule, this one has its exceptions; we'll address these as they occur in the workshop sessions.

Italian soft glass is readily available and comes in a wide variety of colors. Clearly, however, one of the fastest growing areas of the beadmaking-supply industry is the increasing availability of glass that competes favorably with Italian soft glass—glass with the same COE and in additional colors. Newer types of glass that are saturated with metals such as silver or that have interesting reduction properties are also available. The creative beadmaker can use the quirky aspects of these types of glass to explore new color combinations and glass reactions. Remember: there are entire lines of glass in different COEs. Feel free to execute these bead projects in virtually any kind of soft glass, but make sure that all the glass you use in a single bead has the same COE.

The glass rod colors used to make the workshop beads in this book are specified in the Tools and Materials lists that are included within the workshop sessions. Unless there's a dimension specified for a rod, you can assume that it's 5 to 6 mm in diameter. I prefer German glass for encasing because it's less prone than Italian clear glass to bubble in the flame or become sooty, but use whatever clear glass works best for you and your equipment.

BEAD RELEASE

Page after page could be dedicated to the subject of *bead release*, the clay-like substance that we use to coat our mandrels and that permits the bead first to stick to the mandrel and then to release from it after annealing. Many brands of bead release are available, and every beadmaker has his or her favorite. I use a flame-dry bead release; I can dip a mandrel in it, dry it immediately in the flame, and then make a bead. Typically, I let my mandrels dry overnight anyway, and I don't flame dry them, but it's nice to have that option.

Flame drying seems to be least successful on hollow mandrels or mandrels larger than 3/32 inch (2.4 mm) in diameter; dry these overnight if you can. If you're making larger beads or working with fatter mandrels for the first time, try a bead release with superior holding power, whether or not it's flame dryable. Even though the bead may be tough to remove, it will be less likely to break free of the release while you're working in the flame. One further note: I make many transparent beads, so I'm fond of a bead release that doesn't mar the smooth holes in them.

Bead release on mandrels

WORKSTATION

Everyone should work in settings that are comfortable and safe for them. I'm tall, so my chair is a desk chair that I can raise high enough to plant both feet comfortably flat on the floor. I don't usually use armrests, but while I'm working, I try to remember to sit up straight and keep my shoulders and arms relaxed. I take breaks after every bead, if only to stretch, wiggle my fingers, and drink some water.

I assemble all of my materials for a bead before I begin. Nonetheless, sometimes a creative impulse strikes, and I need to grab more glass, materials, or tools. For this reason, everything in my studio is only about one step away from my seat. My kiln is also close by in case I need to access components I've garaged, as is the case in the Rose Bead (pages 114–119) or return an annealed and reheated bead to the flame, as we do in the Beach Bead (pages 26–33). For some beads, I place a hot plate on my worktable. Because the lighting in my studio is a little uneven, I have a halogen desk lamp that I can pull over to light my work.

My studio bench, cleaned up for visitors

Annealing

A great deal has been written on the subject of *annealing*—the controlled cooling of a bead to eliminate internal stress that would otherwise be present in the glass. As a result, some confusing and contradictory information has made its way into the brains of beadmakers. Annealing can't be done without a *kiln* (sometimes referred to as an "oven"), the temperature of which is monitored by a thermometer called a "pyrometer," and it can't be done without slowly reducing the temperature over a period of several hours. Cooling a hot bead in a fiber blanket or in a tub of vermiculite (or something similar to vermiculite) is just that—cooling. Beads cooled in this manner but not annealed will quite possibly crack at some point.

Small beads that have been cooled in the coolest part of the torch flame (a process sometimes referred to as "flame annealing") can usually survive further cooling in a fiber blanket without cracking. In many instances, after several small beads have been cooled to room temperature, they can be placed in a cold kiln, slowly brought up to the annealing temperature for that particular glass, held there for a defined period of time, and slowly cooled to achieve true annealing. This so-called "batch annealing" will work for some, but not all, of the beads in this book. Most of the workshop sessions, however, are based on the assumption that you have a kiln nearby and can pop an individual hot bead into it as soon as you've completed it in the torch.

The more advanced techniques that some of these workshop beads entail require more critical control of the heat applied to the bead and to bead components such as the candy cane on the Wreath Bead (pages 90–96). Thus a

The little doggie door on my kiln allows me to add beads all day long while the kiln holds at annealing temperature.

large bead such as the Beach Bead (pages 26–33) would be difficult to cool successfully in a fiber blanket; its size, slim profile, and copper inclusions all make the bead more susceptible to thermal shock.

The kiln shown in the photo on this page is the one I use in my studio. Its little doggie-style door allows me to insert hot beads into the kiln without opening the lid. The lid does open, however, and that will be an important feature when we talk about manipulating beads in and out of the kiln, and bending beads (pages 26–33 and 109–111). I set the kiln's controller to maintain a temperature of 965°F (518°C) until I've placed the last bead of the day in the kiln. Assuming that the last bead is a large, focal one, the kiln stays at 965°F (518°C) for one more hour. It then cools at a rate of 100°F (38°C) per hour until it reaches 850°F (454°C), where it holds for one hour. It then continues to cool at a rate of 300°F (149°C) per hour to 400°F (204°C), at which point it shuts off automatically and slowly cools to room temperature.

Safety

Many of the daily activities of our lives are unsafe if we're careless or lack adequate knowledge. That's why we don't use blow-dryers when we're standing in bathtubs and why we don't let small children drive our family cars. Although blow-dryers and cars can both be used safely, they need to be used carefully and by people who know how to operate them. Which brings us to safe beadmaking. Beginning beadmakers should take the time to obtain the information that will enable them to set up safe beadmaking studios and to work safely with glass and torches. As advanced beginners or intermediate students, a short review of the highlights attendant to safe practice is never a bad idea. The overview that follows is merely a reminder; it isn't a substitute for the knowledge that beginners must acquire in order to work safely.

STUDIO SETUP

A safe studio should have a heatproof surface on the floor and on the worktable. The wooden tables in my studio are covered with sheets of steel from the hardware store. My floor and walls are cement. You can purchase fireproof fabrics to cover almost any type of floor; these fabrics are used frequently in beadmaking teaching venues such as conference centers, where bits of glass might ignite the carpeting. Don't ignore the surface under the kiln; stone or ceramic tile from a home center is an excellent choice there. Observe the kiln manufacturer's advice about placing the kiln a safe distance from walls and other flammable surfaces.

My kiln, tools, and glass are adjacent to my studio bench.

Keep a bowl of water on your work surface and a fire extinguisher nearby. The bowl is handy for quenching tools or disposing of bits of hot glass as you work, but in a pinch, it's also the first thing that you could dump on a flame. Naturally, if a fire broke out, you'd want to use a fire extinguisher as quickly as possible, which is why it should be easily accessible and fully charged (fire extinguishers don't last forever).

Another handy safety feature is a *quick disconnect*, which connects the torch's hose to the regulator; in the event of fire, it's usually the fastest way to separate the supply of fuel from the torch—and thus stop fueling the flames. Your torch should be clamped or bolted to the table so that you don't accidentally knock it onto the floor or into your lap. I like to use a clamp because it allows me to reposition the torch as necessary for different tasks.

Always secure tanks of oxygen so they can't be knocked over. If an oxygen tank is knocked to the ground and its valve is dislodged, the tank becomes a missile due to the pressurized gas that's expelled from it through the narrow hole at its top. Just as a filled balloon will fly around a room if you release the air in it quickly, a tank of oxygen will move around as it expels its pressurized load. Obviously, this can be extremely dangerous. Gas-supply companies sell bases that will hold tanks in place. Alternatively, you can chain a tank to a wall.

Oxygen tanks can be stored indoors, but the safest place for propane tanks is outdoors. In the United States, propane tanks are now fitted with safety valves that are supposed to prevent leaks. Leaks can still happen, however, and since propane is highly flammable, it's very dangerous to keep the tank inside your house. An outdoor tank can temporarily supply gas through a hose that passes through an open window or a hole in a wall. My propane tank is in a shed about 20 feet (6.1 m) away from my house. The propane is fed into my studio through an underground hose inside a pipe that runs through the studio wall. This is a pretty elaborate arrangement, but once it was set up, it was heavenly.

VENTILATION

Adequate studio ventilation is a must. A torch is indiscriminate; it gobbles up not only the oxygen that is fed to it through its hose, but also the oxygen in the room—the oxygen that you were counting on being able to inhale. Stale, oxygen-deprived air should be drawn out of the room and replaced with fresh air; in addition to an exhaust fan, your studio should have a door or window through which replacement air can arrive.

Depending on the materials you choose to use when you make beads, ventilation may be especially important. Exposure to metal fumes (from gold or silver, for example); lead fumes (from certain glasses and frits); and carbon monoxide (a byproduct of the torch) is very unhealthy. Good ventilation will pull these fumes away from your face and out of your work area, and allow the air to be replaced continuously.

CLOTHING AND EYE PROTECTION

Choose clothes and a hairstyle appropriate for your work. All beadmakers are aware of the fact that sometimes cold rods that are hurried into a hot flame will spit bits of glass. For this reason, I encourage students to point the hot end of the rod at the work surface until the rod has started to melt. Nonetheless, bits of glass do fly around at times, so wear clothing that covers as much of your body as possible (especially your arms and chest) and that's made of a natural fiber that won't melt or catch fire easily. Also keep long hair tied back and out of the way.

Whenever you manipulate hot glass in the kiln, or remove heated beads or bead components from a hot kiln, wear heat-resistant gloves or mitts, and sleeves that will protect your skin and clothes. These are usually

The correct eyewear will protect you from the flare of the glass in the flame and from rare flying bits of glass.

available from the hot-glass supply companies that sell kilns. Remember, when you open a kiln, the first air that whooshes out is air heated to kiln temperature; in other words, it's truly hot. Even if you don't place your hand inside the kiln, you need to protect yourself from the heated air that emanates from it.

Beadmaking requires special eyewear. I've always felt strongly that safety glasses with lampworking filters are the wisest choice for torchwork; purchase yours from a reputable dealer—and make sure you wear them. If your torch glasses keep sliding down your nose or distort the prescription glasses you wear under them, figure out a way to tie them in place. You need both hands to make beads, and glasses always seem to slip at the most critical moments in the most complex beadmaking processes. I wear eyeglass frames that are designed for use in a chemistry lab. The bottom portion of the frame, closest to my face, contains my prescription lenses; on top of those lenses is a second flip-up frame that holds my filtered lenses. If I need to look at something without the filter, I can flip the upper frame up and out of the way, and then pull it down again when I'm ready to return to the torch. Safety glasses come in many configurations; just make sure your eyes are well protected.

RESPIRATORS

Good ventilation isn't a substitute for a respirator, which should always be worn when you work with dusts or particulates such as enamels, *pixie dust* (or powdered mica), and reduction powders. Beadmakers also need protection from the fumes that result from the application of metals such as gold, silver, and palladium;

purchase an appropriate cartridge respirator for these tasks. These are available in home stores, they aren't expensive, and the cartridges are replaceable. If you're only handling enamels and powders, an inexpensive particulate respirator, which looks a bit like a common dust mask, will do, but a cartridge respirator is your safest bet—one rated by the United States NIOSH (The National Institute for Occupational Safety and Health) as at least N-100. Keep in mind that enamels and pixie dust can become airborne; clean them up with damp paper towels and dispose of the towels in closed containers.

Remember that your safety is your own responsibility. Beadmaking, like many other enjoyable activities, can't be done mindlessly. Fire, heat, and glass, with which you can produce fascinating, beautiful, and useful works of art, are all inherently dangerous. If you develop good safety-related habits in your studio, you'll find that the accommodations you have to make will never outweigh the benefits of the artistic results you can achieve.

How to Use This Book

The workshop sessions that follow are based on the notion that by using photos and written instructions, I can teach you the skills and techniques that I ordinarily teach in my actual workshops. Each of the ten sessions introduces one finished bead; the tools, materials, and techniques required to make that bead; and a description of each step that's taken to complete it—more or less what I offer in a class. (I start with the easiest beads and move on to more challenging ones.) I also include in each session a section titled Further Explorations. Here you'll find one or more variations on the main bead theme, descriptions of how to make these variations, and useful information about tools and materials that will help you to create variations of your own. The tools and materials necessary for these variations are described in the instructions rather than listed, so be sure to read the instructions before you begin.

One way to approach the beads presented is to gather the materials and tools that you learn about in any given session, and then attempt to copy the bead as a way of mastering the techniques that making it entails. Ah—if you were paying attention as you read the last sentence, you'll have noticed that I used the dreaded word, "copying." Among beadmakers, there's much debate about whether anyone owns a particular technique or design, and, if so, whether another beadmaker should use that technique or design in his or her beads, or whether doing so is merely copying. For the purposes of this book, I invite you to copy my designs and to learn new skills through the copying process. No one's forcing you

to copy these beads, however, which brings me to another way in which you can use this book: Read about the materials, tools, and techniques that are of interest to you; then combine them to create your own beads. This approach won't leave you with a series of finished, well-executed designs until you've mastered the techniques you've chosen to learn. It will, however, move your own body of work forward by incorporating fresh information and tools.

I've also included photo galleries of work by other artists to further demonstrate some of the same building blocks that I've used in my workshop beads. As you'll see, these artists have used identical or similar techniques to

Smoothing a hollow bead in the flame

produce results quite different from my own interpretations. These photographs represent variations on the theme of the workshop session in which they're found, and are meant to tempt you to push the envelope of your own beadmaking and to strike out in new and creative directions. Copying my work is fine at first, but in order to find your voice as an artist and beadmaker, you should strive to use the same materials, tools, and techniques available to everyone else, but in ways that result in your own unique expressions of creativity.

Every painter paints with the same colors as every other artist, every composer composes with the same notes as every other musician, and every beadmaker uses the same basic materials. It's each artist's individual voice that differentiates one painting, piece of music, or bead from the others. Your artistic voice is as unique as your fingerprint; your challenge is to express your own voice in a way that's different from every other beadmaker. My humble goal is to provide you with exercises in the form of beads that will help you identify and strengthen your creative voice so that it becomes a distinct creative presence, different from all the rest.

Falling Leaves Bead

Perfect worn alone as a pendant or as part of a floral or autumnal necklace, this lovely bead appears more complex than it is. Creating it is just a matter of taking several simple steps.

What Will This Session Teach?

Here we'll explore the versatility of copper and the quirky nuances that can be achieved in its color by experimenting with heat. This bead is an excellent entry-level sandblasting project, too; the simple, repetitive design is blasted into the glass surface—not through a layer of enamel, as in the Beach Bead (pages 26–33). Making this bead will also introduce you to the use of dichroic-coated glass.

GENERAL TOOLS AND MATERIALS

Glass rods:

  Transparent teal

  Clear glass

Basic tools (page 11)

Torch-mounted marver (optional)

Sharp, pointed tweezers

SPECIAL TOOLS AND MATERIALS

Copper foil, lightweight (40 gauge)

Paper punches

Dichroic-coated clear glass

Masking material

Sandblasting equipment

Solvent (gum and tar remover)

Vinyl protectant

(A) Copper foil, (B) glass rods, (C) dish of dichroic-coated glass strips, (D) copper-foil leaf cutouts in dish and on benchtop marver, and (E) paper punches in leaf shapes

Notes on Specialty Tools and Materials

Let's begin by discussing the special tools and materials you'll need for the Falling Leaves Bead.

Copper foil, lightweight (40 gauge): To make the leaf-shaped copper inclusions, you'll use commercial paper punches or scissors to cut the shapes from a sheet of copper foil—the kind that's sold for embossing—in the lightest weight available.

Dichroic-coated clear glass: When purchasing this glass, also referred to as "dichro glass," be wary of bargains. The higher-priced glass available from established lampwork suppliers is better in quality than some of the dichro glass suitable for fusing and is better able to withstand the heat of the flame. For greater ease of use and aesthetic success, I prefer to purchase a ½-inch-wide (1.3 cm) dichro strip that's been slightly slumped in a kiln. (*Slumping* is the process of gently heating the strips in the kiln so that their edges begin to round slightly.) These slumped strips are readily available, but if you like, you can purchase a larger piece of dichro, cut it to the desired size, and slump it in your own kiln. Dichroic coating is available on many different types of glass; make sure the dichro you purchase is compatible with the glass you plan to use in your bead (see Glass on page 12).

Masking material: Before you sandblast a design onto a bead, you'll apply a masking material (or "resist") to protect the areas of the bead that won't be blasted. The easiest-to-use materials are commercially available stickers; the best for sandblasting are precisely cut on heavy metallic paper. This is one reason why beadmakers haunt the scrapbooking aisles in craft stores. For the unique designs on this bead, however, you'll cut the masking from the vinyl sheets that are sold for commercial sign making. The vinyl can be punched, or cut with a craft knife or scissors.

Sandblasting equipment: See Appendix A on pages 126–129.

Vinyl protectant: Manufactured for dashboards and tires, this product adheres to etched glass and reduces its whitish surface to a pleasing frost.

An Overview

We'll begin this asymmetrical bead by making a skinny tube and wrapping it with dichro glass. Then we'll dot copper leaves onto the dichro and encase them in a heavy layer of clear glass. The last steps are masking the cooled bead with leaf-shaped pieces of vinyl strategically placed over the copper leaves, and sandblasting.

Creating the Bead

Making the Leaves
Use paper punches to cut out several different copper-foil leaves. I usually punch more than I need so that I can piece them onto the bead's surface in any combination that appeals to me. Arrange the leaves on a torch-mounted marver or as close to the torch as possible (photo 1).

Winding the Base Bead
Wind a transparent teal tube bead onto the mandrel, approximately 1½ inches (3.8 cm) long. Keep the tube as skinny as possible (photo 2); this bead tends to grow with the addition of each layer.

Introduce the uncoated side of the dichro strip into

the edge of the coolest part of the flame. While warming the first 1 inch (2.5 cm) of it, heat the very tip so that it will adhere to the tube (photo 3). Preheat a spot at one end of the tube (this will be the top of the bead) and

attach the dichro strip at an angle, with the dichro-coated surface face down (photo 4). Using gentle heat directed primarily at the uncoated surface of the strip, soften the

strip so that it adheres to the bead and spirals around it (photo 5). *Don't* heat the strip to the molten stage until after you've completed the next step (sealing its edges). If

you heat the strip too much now, its edges will curl upward toward its center, exposing the dichroic-coated surface to the flame and causing an unattractive grey scum to form.

Before heating the bead's surface to achieve its ultimate shape, you must spread the transparent glass on the top surface of the dichro strip over the strip's edges to seal in the dichro coating. Heat one small portion along the length of the strip's edge, and use a knife or tweezers to push the heated glass over the edges of the dichroic coating (photo 6). Repeat to seal all the edges, along the entire length of the strip.

workshop*wisdom*

Occasionally, despite your best efforts to seal dichro-coated edges, a thin line of scum forms where you've heated too aggressively before spreading the clear over the edges of the dichro coating, or where you've failed to spread the glass quite enough. The Falling Leaves Bead is forgiving; the scum won't show in the finished product. Nonetheless, if you see any scum, now's a good time to practice removing it by spot-heating it with a direct flame and pinching it off with pointed tweezers.

Now heat the bead enough to shape it, and using a handheld marver, bring the bead to a slightly conical shape (photo 7). This shape will become more pronounced after you've added the leaves.

Applying the Leaves

I like to orient the copper leaves so that they appear to be floating downward. In order to vary the colors of the copper in the finished bead, we'll apply the leaves in three different ways.

Method One: While keeping the base bead warm, gather the end of the rod of clear. While you're heating the spot where the leaf will be applied, push the molten gather of clear down onto a copper leaf (photo 8); then use the rod

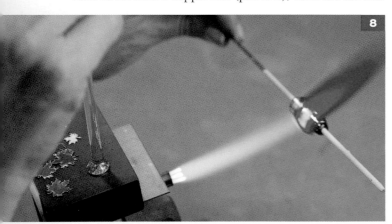

to adhere the leaf to the bead (photo 9). *Don't* try to pull the rod away from the bead. Instead, direct the flame at the junction where the rod meets the bead, and burn the rod off (photo 10). To make sure the copper leaf is thoroughly encased in clear glass, use a marver to press the glass down onto the leaf. If necessary, heat and pluck off any bulky, excess glass on top of the leaf (photo 11).

Method Two: Preheat the base bead and use pointed tweezers to apply the copper leaf (photo 12). Then encase the leaf with clear glass. The bead's brief exposure to the heat of encasing will turn the copper color ruddier.

Method Three: Preheat the base bead and use pointed tweezers to apply the leaf. After making sure that the entire underside of the leaf has made contact with the surface of the bead, liberally heat the copper (photo 13); then encase it in clear glass. If the leaf isn't in full contact with the bead's surface, the heat of the flame will melt and deform it—an effect that can be interesting. When the bead comes out of the kiln, the leaf colors will range from deep rust to bright copper, depending on the

amount of heat they received before encasing. (My thanks go to beadmaker Jill Symons for having taught me this trick.)

Add additional clear glass as needed and finish shaping the bead (photo 14).

Sandblasting the Bead

After the bead is annealed and cooled, carefully remove the excess bead release from around it while it's still on the mandrel; use a damp paper towel to avoid creating dust. Wipe the bead off thoroughly. (Handle it as little as possible afterward; oil from your hands will interfere with the adhesion of the vinyl resist.)

Using the paper punches or a craft knife, cut leaves from the vinyl resist and apply them to the bead as masks (photo 15). Sandblast the bead while it's on the mandrel (see Appendix A on page 126). After sandblasting, the leaf shapes will stand above the sandblasted surface (photo 16). I prefer a deep etch so that the leaves are in

sharp relief to the frosted background, but by all means play with this variable as you shape your design (photo 17). Soak the bead in warm water to remove the resist.

Remove the bead from the mandrel. When it's dry, clean off any remaining adhesive with a solvent (a product made to remove chewing gum, grease, and tar works well). Then clean and dry the bead again to remove the solvent. As the last step, I usually buff sandblasted beads with a coat of vinyl protectant to remove the whitish frost that's left by the sandblasting.

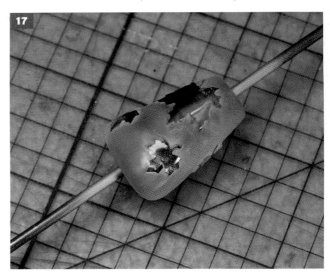

Further Explorations

DRAGONFLY BEADS

Dichroic-coated glass and sandblasting are elements in a finished bead that greatly complement each other. As you can see in the photo above, simply varying the depth of the encasing or the depth of the sandblast etching can yield vastly different but equally appealing results.

The cores of both these Dragonfly Beads are transparent glass. In the rainbow bead, that core is clear and is covered with a rainbow-patterned dichro (photo 18). The uncoated side of this dichro is the only encasing; the dragonfly is sandblasted into it. In the bright blue bead, the core is transparent dark amethyst. The dichro is a pink/teal color and is further encased by a layer of clear encasing glass; the dragonfly design is sandblasted into that encasing layer. Vinyl was used as a masking material on both beads.

18

On a round bead, allover coverage with a sandblasted pattern can be tricky because it requires blasting around curves.

BARBARA BECKER SIMON

Splat Bead, 2003
1 x 1⅛ inch (2.5 x 2.9 cm) in diameter
Gold fumed; sandblasted; hollow work; soda-lime glass
Photo by Rob Stegmann

These sandblasted patterns are made visually interesting by the patterned cores of the beads.

JAYNE LeRETTE

It's a Blast!, 2006
Various sizes
Sandblasted; soft glass
Photo by artist

The vivid copper wire, mesh, and foil inclusions in these simple beads all serve to radiate reflected light.

JILL A. SYMONS

Electric Raspberry Rounds, 2007
Each, ½ inch (1.3 cm) in diameter
Encased; soft glass; copper wire;
copper mesh; copper foil
Photo by artist

The beauty of this sandblasted leaf pattern is enhanced by the use of multiple beads and the repetition of the leaf theme.

NEIL FABRICANT

Untitled, 2005
¾ x ½ inch (1.9 x 1.3 cm)
Lampworked; masked; sandblasted;
soda-lime glass; Czech glass beads;
copper leaves; findings
Necklace designed by Ronnie Lambrou
Photo by artist

Beach Bead

This focal bead conveys the tranquility of a lazy day at the beach or the serenity of a distant vista. It makes a perfect pendant when wire-wrapped and suspended, but its fire-polished surface feels so good that you may want to keep it in your pocket and use it as a worry stone on those days when tranquility and serenity seem too far away.

What Will This Session Teach?

This bead includes a wealth of techniques: incorporating copper, applying enamel, using a specialty bead press, and sandblasting. Because it's a long, thin bead, it will also challenge your heat-control skills. In spite of its name, the Beach Bead is no day at the beach to make!

GENERAL TOOLS AND MATERIALS

Glass rods:

Transparent light blue

Transparent cobalt blue

Clear, 8 mm in diameter

Basic tools (page 11)

Sharp, pointed tweezers

Plain white paper and pencil

Craft knife or scissors

Self-healing mat (optional)

Large, serrated tweezers

SPECIAL TOOLS AND MATERIALS

Specialty bead press

Copper foil, lightweight (40 gauge)

Paper punch

Powdered enamels

Enamel sifters

Masking material

Sandblasting equipment

Solvent (gum and tar remover)

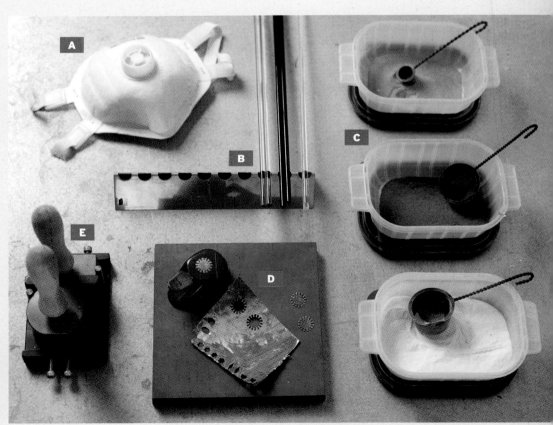

(A) Particulate respirator, (B) glass rods, (C) powdered enamels with sifters, (D) benchtop marver with copper foil and punch, and (E) specialty bead presses with base

Notes on Specialty Tools and Materials

We'll begin by discussing the special tools and materials you'll need for the Beach Bead.

Specialty bead press: Brass specialty presses are available in many shapes and from many makers (photo 1). Filling the cavity of one with the same amount of glass each time usually results in beads of the same size and shape. Presses are especially helpful for forming symmetrical, *tabulated* (flattened) beads. The press we'll use here has the advantageous feature of allowing the artist to form beads of almost unlimited length. If you don't have access to a press like this one, you can tabulate your bead with handheld mashers and shape it with a handheld marver; just use these alternatives as opportunities to play with creating a new and different shape.

Copper foil, lightweight (40 gauge): See page 20.

Powdered enamels: This bead includes three opaque enamel colors: white for the clouds and the crests of the waves, and blue and green for the water. The available palette of enamel colors can be used to vary and expand the usual color palette of glass, but remember to use enamels that are compatible with your glass. Here, we're going to use a line of enamels that's been formulated specifically for the 104 COE glass used in this bead.

Enamel sifters: You'll apply the enamel to this bead with little 1-inch (2.5 cm) basket sifters. Remember: Inhaling enamel is unhealthy, so wear a particulate respirator when you're working with enamels or transferring them from one container to another. To clean up any excess, use damp paper towels so that you don't create any unnecessary dust clouds. (For information on other ways to apply enamels, see pages 122–123.)

Masking material: See page 20 for information on the vinyl that's used to mask this bead before sandblasting.

Sandblasting equipment: See Appendix A on pages 126–129. The distinctive patterns of the waves and clouds are sandblasted into the surface of this bead.

An Overview

The initial challenges are forming the lozenge shape from transparent glass and encasing the copper sun in the sky. Next, we'll sift a thin layer of enamel over the surface of the bead to form a base for the water and clouds. After annealing and cooling the bead, we'll mask the shapes of the water and clouds, and sandblast the excess enamel around them to expose the base bead. Then we'll reheat the bead in the kiln, reintroduce it into the flame, and gently fire polish it to soften the sharp angles left by the sandblasting and eliminate the frosty surface of the transparent base glass. Before taking the steps that follow, punch out the copper-foil sun and place it on your torch-mounted marver or on a marver positioned as close to the torch as possible.

Creating the Bead

Making the Base Bead

This two-tone base bead is built as a lozenge shape about 2 inches (5.1cm) long that tapers very slightly at the ends. It's about two-thirds transparent light blue (the sky) and one-third transparent cobalt blue (the ocean). After forming the base bead (photo 2), heat it uniformly so that its temperature is even throughout; it should be glowing hot, but not so hot that it loses its shape.

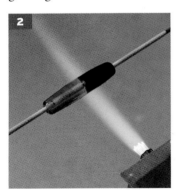

Place the hot bead in the bottom of the press (photo 3), and slowly lower the top part of the press down onto it. Be gentle; if you press too aggressively, you may break the bead release. It may take one or two tries at heating and pressing to achieve a satisfactory shape.

Keep in mind that brass sucks all the heat out of a bead. Before reintroducing the pressed bead into the flame to fire polish it, apply some allover insurance heat to the bead so that its temperature is even throughout.

A specialty press can also leave behind a "chill mark" on the glass, just as any cold tool will do. To remove this, fire polish each face of the bead now, taking care not to soften the taper of the sides by applying direct heat.

Applying the Copper Sun

After applying some insurance heat to the entire bead, gather the end of a rod of clear (photo 4). (Other transparent colors will also work and will affect the tint of the copper.) Because the copper sun shape is large, I use a fat rod of clear, but it's the size of the gather that will matter in the next step.

Two things must now happen simultaneously. While you're heating the spot on the bead where the copper will be applied, you push the molten gather of clear down onto the copper sun (photo 5) and use the rod of clear to apply the sun to the bead (photo 6). *Don't* try to pull the rod away from the bead. Instead, direct the flame at the

junction where the rod meets the bead and burn the rod off (photo 7). Next, heat and pluck off any bulky excess glass on top of the sun (photo 8). Return the bead to its

original lozenge shape by heating the entire side on which you've placed the copper sun, then pressing the bead against the base of the press to reshape it (photo 9). In this bead, I've chosen to preserve the original color of the copper. Take a look at Applying the Leaves in the Falling Leaves Bead session (page 22) for suggestions about changing that color.

In the next step, the application of enamel will obscure the copper sun. Usually, I want to know exactly where the sun is so that I can position a cloud to cover only a part of it. To do this, before going on to add the enamel, I make a small spacer bead on the mandrel, above the base bead, and flatten it. Then I mark the spacer bead with a contrasting dot that lines up with the placement of the sun (photo 10). I use the same technique in the Geode Bead to help me remember where I intend to grind it (see photo 11 on page 43).

Applying the Enamel

Enamel will only stick to a warm bead surface. The bead must be warmer than the coolest part of the flame, but not floppy and molten, so the first step is to warm the bead to about the level of heat that you need to remove chill marks from its surface. Next, hold the bead close to the work surface and use a 1-inch (2.5 cm) basket sifter to sprinkle a thin coat of white enamel over both sides (photo 11). To make the sifter work, just scratch the

twisted wires of its handle with one fingernail. Your goal is to cover the base glass color entirely with the thinnest possible coat of enamel, but several more coats will follow this one, so you don't need to cover the glass completely this time. Pay attention to which end of the bead is the top (the sky) and which is the bottom (the ocean); soon you won't be able to tell by looking.

After the enamel is applied, it appears granular. Slowly and gently heat the entire surface so that the enamel melts and flows to make a smooth coating (photo 12). Try not to use the marver, which presses the enamel

grains into the glass; this will make it harder to create a smooth, sandblasted surface later. If you're rushing and heat the enamel too much, you'll see it boil on the surface—an interesting effect, but not what you want in this bead. Now heat the other side of the bead, sprinkle it with enamel, and smooth the surface.

workshop*wisdom*

For some enamel applications, you can avoid creating extra dust by rolling the bead in a dish or spoon of enamel instead of sifting it. That won't work on this bead, however, because the best sandblasting results depend on even, thin coats of enamel, which are best achieved by sifting.

If you have trouble getting the enamel to adhere to the base bead (sometimes it curdles on the surface), the bead wasn't warm enough. If the bead is getting so cool that the enamel won't stick, it may be in danger of cracking. Take the time to scrape off any loose enamel and thoroughly reheat the bead. Then reapply the enamel.

The next coat of enamel—another coat of white on the top one-third of the bead—will give the sky a nice even coverage for the eventual white clouds. Extending the white out to the edges or to the top hole isn't important. Just visualize where the cloud will be on each side; that's where the bead needs the even coat of white.

After you've applied the second coat of white and melted it smooth, sprinkle the lower two-thirds of the bead, on both sides, with blue enamel and a touch of green enamel. No two oceans look alike, and neither will any two beads. This blue/green coat should completely cover the white on that part of the bead and should also be melted smooth (photo 13).

At this stage, you have a bead that's one-third white and two-thirds blue/green. Reheat the bead, warming it evenly throughout, and pop it into the kiln to anneal in the usual manner. The enamel surface is slightly softer than the Italian glass, so if you place other beads in the kiln, be careful not to let them touch the surface of the enameled bead.

Coldworking the Bead

When the bead has cooled to room temperature, break away all the bead release from around it without moving it on the mandrel and being careful not to inhale any dust. If the bead is loose, tape it onto another mandrel (page 129). Make sure the bead's surface is clean and dry. Once it is, try not to touch the enamel; oil from your hands will prevent the vinyl resist from sticking to it.

On a piece of plain white paper, develop patterns for the clouds (one for each side of the bead); then place the paper on top of a sheet of vinyl and cut around the patterns. I prefer to use a craft knife on a self-healing mat, but scissors will work, too. Peel the protective backing from the two vinyl cloud elements and adhere them to the bead, noting the location of the sun as you position them. The copper sun will shine on both the front and back of this bead; each view will have a different look and feel.

After you've applied the vinyl-resist elements for the clouds, sandwich the lower portion of the bead, over the ocean, between two pieces of vinyl resist, pinching them tightly around the edges of the bead and extending them onto the mandrel. Use a craft knife to carve the wave shapes through the surface of the vinyl (photo 14).

If you'd rather not cut freehand, prepare cardboard templates of the waves, set them on the vinyl, and cut around them as though they were little pattern pieces. Remember: All exposed areas will be sandblasted away and the glass underneath revealed.

workshop*wisdom*

If a resist material doesn't stick to enameled glass, first make sure the bead is clean and dry. If that doesn't work, after applying the resist, try holding the masked bead under a warm lamp; the heat can help soften the resist's adhesive. If the enamel wasn't melted smooth, its granular structure may be interfering. Try burnishing the resist by rubbing it onto the bead with the flat surface of a metal tool or butter knife.

Sandblast both surfaces of the bead so that all the exposed enamel is removed and only the frosted surface of the bead remains (photo 15). (For information on sandblasting, see Appendix A on pages 126–129.) Then

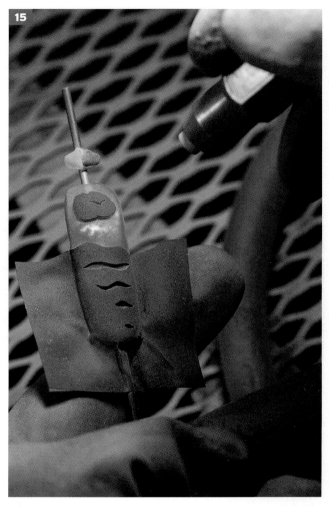

peel off the resist and while the bead is still on the mandrel, thoroughly clean its surface with damp paper towels, using a solvent if necessary. If you're happy with the details of the waves at this stage, you can move on to the final reheating. If you'd like to add more detail, use a handheld, electric jewelry drill to carve away portions of the waves. Because there's a thin layer of white under the blue, a little carving will create white caps on the waves. Similarly, to add contrast and depth, you can drill into the body of the waves, either down to the white layer or even farther down, into the cobalt blue glass underneath. Clean the bead thoroughly again, removing all the resist adhesive and any dust.

Fire Polishing the Bead

Place the bead in a cold kiln, leaving about one-third of the mandrel outside. Heat the bead, bringing it up to approximately 1000°F (538°C) over the next hour and leaving it at that temperature for another 30 minutes. Light your torch and use large tweezers to remove the bead from the kiln. Dip the mandrel into a cup of water so that it's comfortably cool to hold (photo 16); then introduce the bead to the coolest part of the flame.

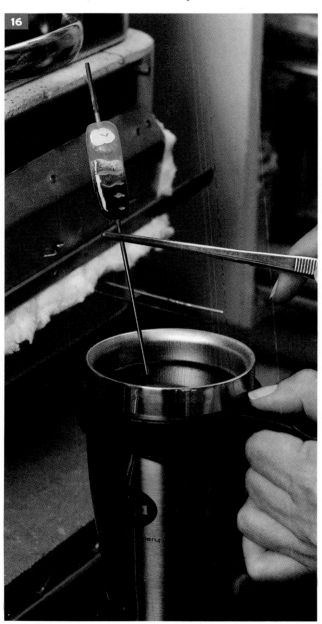

Slowly warm both sides of the bead in the cool tip of the flame; then advance the bead into the heat of the flame (photo 17). The kiln was 1000°F (538°C); the flame is considerably hotter, so you have to give the bead a chance to get hot through and through. In the hottest part of the flame, fire polish the sandblasted surface. Don't rotate the bead in the hot flame, or it will begin to lose its tabular shape. Instead, work on one side and then the other. Not only will the glass become shiny, but the cut edges of the enamel will soften. Reduce the heat if any of the enamel is boiling. To fire polish small crevices or curves, make sure the bead is warm throughout; then increase the oxygen to the torch to create a small flame that comes to a point. Use this pointed flame to spot-heat specific areas. This kind of flame won't keep the bead from cracking, so remember to re-warm it frequently.

When you're satisfied with the fire-polished appearance of the bead, return it to the kiln and anneal as usual.

Further Explorations

HEART BEADS

The Heart Beads shown above illustrate the effects of both sandblasting and the process of *fuming*, which is heating a metal (in this case gold) to the point at which it gives off metal-laden vapors that adhere to the bead. Each base bead, made of a saturated transparent color, is first shaped into a flattened heart and then fumed. Remember to take all appropriate safety precautions when using this technique.

After making the base bead, melt the tip of a rod of borosilicate glass or quartz in the hottest spot in the flame, and place a small piece of 24-karat gold shot or wire on the molten glass (photo 18).

18

In order for the gold fumes to fuse into the bead's surface, the bead should be evenly warm, but not close to glowing hot. Unfortunately, you won't know for sure if the bead was too hot or too cold until it comes out of the kiln; if it was, the gold will come off the bead while you're cleaning it. With practice, you'll learn to recognize just how warm the bead must be to make the gold stick.

Hold the bead in the back of the flame and introduce the gold on the end of the rod into the cones at the base of the flame. Keep the rod upright; as the gold becomes molten, it will roll off the rod and onto the table, or worse yet, into your lap. A change in the flame color to a greenish tinge tells you that the fumes are traveling with the heat of the flame; you can then position the bead in the heart of the fumes, which is usually near the outer tip of the flame (photo 19). Depending on the base color of your bead and how extensively you fume it, gold can add a reflective surface, a slight golden shimmer, or a deep rosy hue. Fumed gold is particularly lovely on ivory or pale lavender.

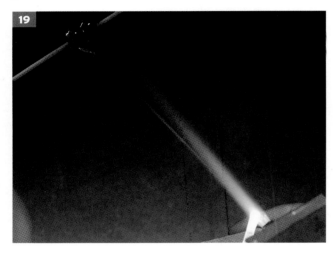

The leaf-and-vine pattern is applied after fuming by using commercially available metallic stickers as sandblasting resists (photo 20). Stickers are more fragile than vinyl resist, but because even a quick sandblasting will remove the thin deposit of gold on the surface of this bead, they'll hold up just fine in this case.

Alternative Sandblasting Resists

In addition to stickers and vinyl masking, another basic type of resist is the liquid product sold to mimic lead lines in craft projects. This comes in a squeeze bottle and is great for masking raised decorations on a bead's surface (such as dots), or the lip of a vessel or its handles.

A more technically challenging resist is called "photoresist." The beauty of this resist is that it permits you to import artwork through your computer, develop the resist as if it were film, and apply it to a bead (photo 21). Photoresist can be used with extremely detailed art, but it's more expensive than other readily available resists, requires specialized computer applications, and works

best on flat or slightly rounded surfaces. Despite its limitations for glass beads, however, it's a very exciting material.

Experimenting with Enamels

The Beach Bead (page 26) was made with opaque enamels, but if you buy a sampler, you can play with transparent enamels, as well as with combinations of transparents and opaques. There are also enamel colors that tend to reduce or react with other colors. Some artists have made good use of enamels' tendency to boil to achieve organic combinations. Using metal stencils to create enamel patterns and using sifters in different sizes are also interesting avenues for exploration.

The artists used photo-resist, which is durable, to mask the letters on the enamel layer of this bead, and then sandblasted through that layer to reveal the glass beneath.

NEIL FABRICANT AND JERI WARHAFTIG

I Am My Beloved's and My Beloved Is Mine, 2006
1⅜ inch (3.5 cm) in diameter
Sandblasted; soda-lime glass; enamel
Photo by David Orr

Before sandblasting, only the fine silver layer on the exterior of this bead was visible, but masking and sandblasting exposed the dichroic glass core, which was then fire polished.

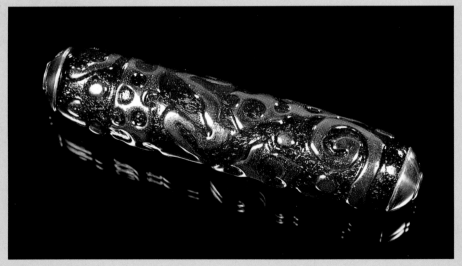

BRONWEN HEILMAN

Untitled, 2002
3 x ¾ inches (7.5 x 1.7 cm) in diameter
Sandblasted; flame polished; dichroic glass; fine silver overlay; sterling silver end caps
Photo by David Orr

Extensive advanced planning resulted in a deceptively simple and elegant design sandblasted into the speckled enamel bases of these stunning beads.

BARBARA BECKER SIMON

Woven Beads, 2003
Largest, 1 x 1⅛ inches (2.5 x 2.9 cm) in diameter
Lampworked; hollow work; sandblasted;
soda-lime glass; enamel
Photo by Larry Sanders

This bead was first enameled and fumed with gold. Then some of the gold areas were masked and others sandblasted, leaving the golden minarets behind.

DIANA EAST

Aladdin's Palace, 2002
1½ x 1 x ½ inches (3.8 x 2.5 x 1.3 cm)
Gold fumed; masked; sandblasted;
etched; dichroic glass; enamel
Photo by artist

DIANA EAST

Oh My God!!!, 2002
1³/₁₆ x 1³/₁₆ x ³/₁₆ inches (3 x 3 x 1 cm)
Flame worked; layered; sandblasted; fire polished;
soda-lime glass; murrini; enamel
Photo by artist

Fire polishing this sandblasted bead brought the transparent glass to a glossy finish and created a window into the whimsical view inside.

Geode Bead

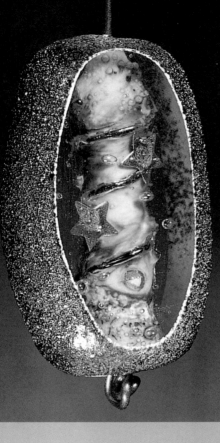

An excellent focal pendant when worn alone, this bead is also lovely displayed on a bead stand in a sunny window. It certainly has its own special "wow" factor—viewers who examine it closely are captivated by its unique miniature world.

What Will This Session Teach?

Making the core bead requires many of the same basic skills as the other beads in this book, but also introduces the fascinating reaction between copper leaf and light-colored enamels, and the use of fine silver wire. The core is a skinny tube of white glass; its turquoise color results from the reaction between the white enamel and copper leaf applied to its surface. The more challenging aspects of this bead include the large amount of encasing, the application of reduction glass powder on the exterior, and the faceting.

GENERAL TOOLS AND MATERIALS

Glass rods:

Opaque white

German clear glass, 5–6 mm in diameter

German clear glass, 8 mm in diameter

Basic tools (page 11)

Sharp, pointed tweezers

Jewelry-size wire cutters

Permanent marker

SPECIAL TOOLS AND MATERIALS

Copper leaf, foil, and wire

Paper punch

Powdered enamel (white)

Enamel sifters

Fine silver wire (20 to 24 gauge)

Reduction glass powder (iris blue)

Flat lap grinder

(A) Benchtop marver with fine silver wire, copper stars, copper wire, pointed tweezers, and copper leaf; (B) jewelry-size wire cutters; (C) glass rods; (D) reduction powder with enamel sifter; (E) copper foil with punch; and (F) powdered enamel with sifter

Notes on Special Tools and Materials

Following is a discussion of the special tools and materials you'll need for the Geode Bead.

Copper leaf, foil, and wire: The core of this bead is embellished with copper leaf, copper wire, and hand-punched copper-foil stars. For more information on copper foil, see page 20. The leaf is available in books of 25 leaves, each 5½ inches (14 cm) square. A quick search in a hardware store should provide you with plenty of wire, which usually comes on a spool. Its gauge isn't critical, but 20- to 22-gauge is ideal. (The higher the number, the thinner the wire.) Although you can apply wire fragments to a bead, starting with a 10-inch-long (25.4 cm) piece and cutting it to size while the bead is at the torch is easiest.

Powdered enamel (white): See page 28.

Enamel sifters: See page 28.

Fine silver wire (20 to 24 gauge): Silver wire is available from jewelry suppliers. Remember to purchase only fine silver wire; sterling won't work. You'll need about 10 inches (25.4 cm) of it.

Reduction glass powder (iris blue): Reduction glass, which is formulated with large amounts of metals relative to typical soda-lime glass recipes, is enjoyed for its only somewhat predictable properties. In a neutral flame—one in which the oxygen and propane are balanced—this glass acts pretty much like any other glass except that it's sometimes reactive and gives unexpected results with certain base colors, such as ivory. However, when it's exposed to a *reducing flame*—one with an excess of propane or natural gas (i.e. an oxygen-starved flame)—the metal oxides come to the surface of the glass and react to produce either a variegation of the glass color or a shiny metallic exterior.

Based solely on its COE, reduction glass is usually incompatible with Italian soft glass, but you'll rarely encounter problems if you use it in small amounts, in the form of frit or powder.

Flat lap grinder: The flat lap grinder and its use are described in Appendix B on pages 130–132.

An Overview

First, we'll cover an enameled bead with copper leaf and embellish it with copper wire, copper-foil stars, and balls of silver wire. Then we'll apply the deep, clear, and clean encasing that facets so beautifully on the grinder. After encasing the bead completely, we'll coat it with more enamel and then reduction powder. Next, we'll reduce the surface, anneal the bead, remove the cooled bead from the mandrel, and clean it. Finally, we'll facet it by grinding and polishing the glass with a flat lap grinder.

Creating the Bead

Applying the White Enamel and Copper Leaf

Prepare by placing the pre-punched copper-foil stars on a torch-mounted or nearby marver, and the enamel in a shallow dish or in an enamel sifter positioned over a container. Tear about one-half sheet of the copper leaf into irregular shapes, holding it with tweezers rather than with your fingers. As is the case with most metallic leaf, copper leaf will adhere to the oil on your hands, although copper leaf isn't as difficult to handle as gold leaf.

workshop *wisdom*

Symmetrical ends and gently puckered holes are elements of well-executed beads. If you're struggling to achieve pleasing results, try building the core bead by starting with two spacer-sized beads. These will be the right and left ends of your core bead. Then wrap the glass of the core between the two spacers. As you shape and finish the bead, try not to overheat the ends, or they'll draw in towards the center of the bead and undo your hard work.

Using the white glass rod, wind a skinny tube bead onto the mandrel, about 1½ inches (3.8 cm) long. (The Geode Bead has a tendency to grow in size as you make it, so be sure to keep this core bead skinny.) Coat the warm bead thoroughly by sifting white enamel onto it (see photo 11 on page 30) or by rolling the bead in a dish of enamel. Using pointed tweezers, pick up fragments of copper leaf and place them on the warmed bead; then burnish them with the flat outer surface of the tweezers. Unlike the gold leaf in the Hollow Vessel Bead (pages

78–84) and the silver leaf in the Bent Bead (pages 109–111), copper leaf won't adhere readily to enamel. Just persevere by pressing it on with the tweezers (photo 1).

The copper will turn black and ashy when it's first heated, but as it reacts with the enamel, it will turn bluish green. Try to apply the leaf in single or at most double layers, but not in layers any thicker. In spots where there are multiple layers of copper, sift on a tad more enamel to ensure the reaction.

Many beadmakers who have tried this technique are so discouraged by the blackened appearance of the copper after it's been introduced into the flame that they stop at this point. However, the blackened look only indicates that no reaction has happened yet. The bead must get much hotter before the enamel and copper will sizzle on its surface (photo 2). Make sure you heat every area

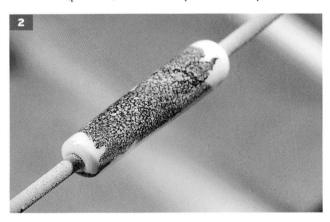

where you've placed the copper on the enamel. If no reaction occurs, you may have missed a spot when you applied the enamel. Just sift a bit more on top of the copper, and then reheat the bead. Sifting on more enamel and reheating will also help if the reaction is insufficient (you'll see black, burned copper that hasn't turned bluish green).

workshop *wisdom*

Sometimes, copper leaf can be reactive with white glass even in the absence of white enamel. This doesn't happen reliably, however, and when the reaction does happen, it doesn't produce as intense a blue color on the finished bead as when the glass has been coated with enamel.

When you use white or light-colored enamel powder on a white core bead, only a light or speckled coat is required. There's no need to worry about how much enamel you apply because any areas left uncovered won't look all that different from areas that are covered. But if you're using an enamel of a different color than your core, you can achieve a variegated color effect by applying the enamel sparingly so the core color will show through in some areas. In the bead shown to the right, the white enamel and copper leaf are on a pale aqua hollow bead.

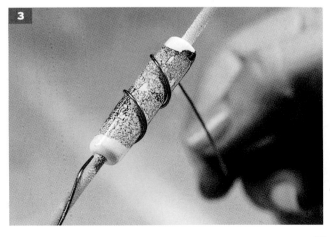

Applying the Copper Wire and Copper-Foil Stars

After the reaction of copper leaf and enamel has taken place on the core bead, hold the mandrel in your non-dominant hand and tuck the end of the 10-inch-long (25.4 cm) piece of copper wire between the thumb of that hand and the mandrel. Wrap the wire onto the bead in a spiral (photo 3). Be careful not to tug too hard on the wire as you wrap it; the end under your thumb can slide and break the bead release. (That's what happened to the first bead I tried to make for this book.) Now use the flame or wire cutters to cut the wire at the end of the bead farthest from your thumb. Even if the wire hasn't adhered to the bead, its spiral shape will hold it around the glass for now.

Heat and marver the bead so that the copper wire adheres to it. The wire may turn black, but like the heated copper in the Falling Leaves Bead (pages 18–23), it will ultimately become a ruddy color.

The stars are applied around the bead in the areas where the base bead is exposed between the copper spirals. Keep the bead warm while you gather the end of the smaller clear rod. Preheat the spot where a star will be placed, press the gather of glass down onto a star (photo 4), and apply the star to the bead. *Don't* pull the rod

away; instead, disconnect it from the star by using the flame to cut through it (photo 5). The enamel-and-white-glass core bead is soupy in consistency; if you pull the clear glass away from the bead, it will take the star and some of the base bead away with it.

Inserting the Silver Globes

The silver wire will heat up and melt quickly, so use your tweezers to hold the wire 6 inches (15.2 cm) or more from the end that you intend to apply to the bead. Preheat a spot on the bead so that it becomes glowing hot. With the bead out of the flame, plunge the tip of the silver wire into the bead (photo 6); then return the bead

to the flame to cut through the wire near the bead's surface. The wire that's left behind will ball up into a globe on the bead's surface. Apply little dots of silver in several spots.

workshop*wisdom*

Fine silver will retain its color when it's encased with German clear glass. When encased with other soda-lime clear glass, the silver sometimes appears to be brass or gold. If you anticipate this effect in a bead, you can use it to your advantage to vary the appearance of the silver.

Encasing the Core

Encasing the bead with clear glass is completed in two stages. First, use clear gathers to fill in the gaps around the wire by pushing the molten glass up against the wire spiral (photo 7). Try to fill the undercuts on either side of

the wire where it contacts the bead; otherwise they'll capture bubbles. If you like bubbles, they won't necessarily be a problem, but because the finished bead will inevitably contain a few anyway, we'll try to eliminate this obvious source of them now.

If your core bead is too hot as you encase it, the turquoise color will swirl and move with the heat of the encasing gathers. The visual result can be attractively celestial, but if you prefer to avoid it, make sure your base bead is warm, not hot.

To finish the encasing, first heat the bead to smooth its surface. (To avoid any soot formation in the clear glass, be sure to use a neutral flame with a little extra oxygen.) Then use a marver to shape the clear glass that's already in place (photo 8). Next, using a molten gather at the end of the 8-mm clear glass rod, add wraps to encase

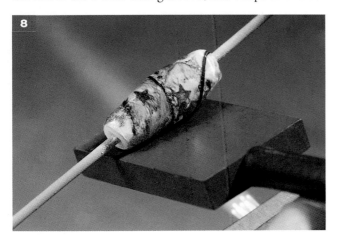

the entire bead. In order to reduce the number of bubbles, make sure the base bead is very warm, but not so hot that it smears, and overlap each wrap of glass slightly over the shoulder of the previous wrap (photo 9). If you see elongated bubbles between the glass wraps, you haven't tucked each wrap tightly enough against the previous one. To make the finished bead slightly egg shaped (photo 10), add a little more encasing around its equator.

Applying More Enamel

The next step will obscure the interior of the bead until you facet it on the flat lap grinder, so take a moment now to study the bead and choose the best front and rear views; they should be opposite one another. Create a spacer bead on the mandrel, about ½ inch (1.3 cm) away from the encased bead. Place two contrasting dots of glass on the spacer bead, aligning them with the encased bead surfaces that you've chosen to be the front and back (photo 11). This marked spacer will prove to be an invaluable guide when it's time to grind the bead. (The same technique is used in the Beach Bead; see photo 10 on page 30.)

Now is also your last chance to significantly refine the shape of the bead. First take a few minutes to reheat the entire bead. (The heat that you introduce here will increase the heat base in the core and will make it much easier to finish the bead's exterior without causing the bead to crack from thermal shock.) Next, heat the outer surface so the enamel will stick. If the bead has become very large, heat and apply the enamel to one-half of it at a time. Then heat all the enamel until it forms a smooth glossy surface. Now you know why we needed a marked spacer to indicate where the bead surfaces should be ground; the interior of the bead isn't visible at this stage (photo 12).

When you grind the bead, this enamel coating will appear as a white strip between the clear encasing and the layer of reduction powder on the exterior of the bead. Its color will make your bead more light reflective than a bead coated solely in reduction powder.

Applying the Reduction Glass Powder

In an effort to achieve an organic look for this bead, I like to apply the reduction powder as a relief on the surface, so I heat it only enough to make it adhere but not enough to melt it smooth. The enamel layer underneath, which tends to be stickier and to melt at a lower heat than normal soda-lime glass, helps in this endeavor.

Begin by heating the enamel surface until it's molten but *not* boiling; then sprinkle the entire bead with a generous layer of reduction powder (photo 13). Reheat

the surface of the bead so that the powder adheres, but isn't melted smooth. If you overheat a particular spot and it becomes too smooth, just sprinkle on more powder and heat the bead a little more.

Reducing the Outer Layer

Reducing the layer of reduction powder will bring a shimmering metallic finish to the blue exterior of the bead. This final step at the torch has to be the last step because once you've reduced this layer, any reintroduction into a neutral flame will reverse the reduction effect.

Reducing isn't a science, but in general, you'll want to turn the oxygen down so that it's nearly absent from the flame and increase the propane to make the flame approximately 15 inches (38.1 cm) long. Hold the bead far from the torch and bathe it in the propane flame (photo 14); you should see the metal appear. If you don't, try turning off the oxygen entirely or moving to a different area of the flame. As the bead cools, the propane

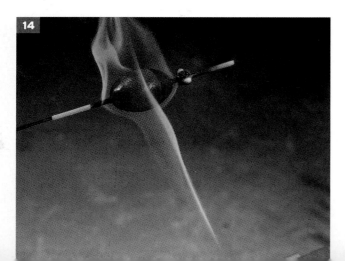

flame will deposit soot on it. This isn't a problem (the soot will come off in the kiln), but once it appears, you've passed the point at which any more reduction will take place. Place the bead in the kiln—and heave a sigh of relief. You've made a huge bead.

Grinding and Polishing the Bead

Before removing the bead from the mandrel, use a permanent marker to transfer the placement of the dots on the spacer bead to the surface of the reduction powder (photo 15). Remove the bead from the mandrel, and clean and dry it.

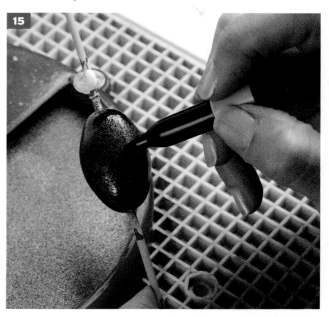

With the flat lap grinder (see Appendix B on pages 130–132), grind the two faces of the bead, using the transferred dots as guides. Use the grinding disks in the following order: 100 grit, 325 grit, 600 grit, and 1200 grit. After you've finished grinding the two faces, use a felt pad charged with cerium oxide to polish them to a high shine (photo 16).

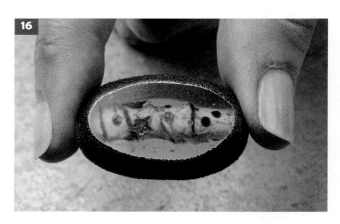

Further Explorations

POLISHED BULL'S-EYE BEAD

The Polished Bull's-Eye Bead shown below is designed to be worn, but like the Geode Bead, can also make a lovely suncatcher. It's created with the same disk-building skills covered in the Blown Hollow Bead session (pages 56–61) and also makes interesting use of enamel.

There's little more to making this bead than applying successive wraps of glass, interspersed with applications of enamel between colors (photo 17). I used a large mandrel, ½ inch (1.3 cm) in diameter (photo 18). (I prefer to allow the bead release on large mandrels to air-dry overnight, even when it's technically flame dryable, since doing so seems to add to the durability of the release.) The bead is almost three times thicker before grinding and polishing than it is afterward (photo 19).

After the bead is annealed, removed from the mandrel, and cleaned, it is coldworked, using the same grinding and polishing processes as we used to facet the Geode Bead. (Photo 20 shows the ground but unpolished bead.) The biggest problem you'll encounter is hanging on to the relatively small, thin piece of glass as you press it against the grinding wheels. Wearing finger cots can help you keep a better grip on it.

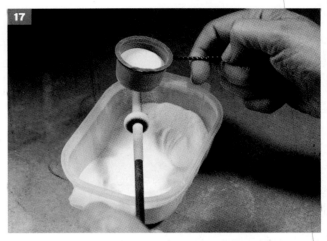

LOUISE MEHAFFEY

Window Bead, 2006

1¾ x ¾ x ½ inches (4.2 x 1.9 x 1.4 cm)

Lampworked; coldworked; soda-lime glass; reduction frit; enamels; fine silver wire; sterling findings and chain

Photo by Jerry Anthony

This well-executed geode bead makes a stunning pendant. The windows in it allow light to pass through the clear encasing, ensuring that the core is highly visible.

Each vessel's upper portion, made of layers of transparent glass, was faceted to create the lovely illusion of a bottle stopper.

LEAH FAIRBANKS

Multi-floral & Gladiolus Vessel, Browneyed Susan & Iris Vessel, and Gladiolus Vessel, 2002

Largest, 2½ inches (6.7 cm) in height

Lampworked; soda-lime glass; handmade cased canes; enamel; silver and gold foil; copper mesh; hand-faceted tops by Derek Lusk

Photo by Robert K. Liu

The borosilicate glass (a very hard glass) used in this bead made faceting especially challenging.

LAURI COPELAND

Rocky Terrain (Multi-Facet), 2006
2⅜ x ½ inches (6 x 1.5 cm)
Encased; ground; polished; borosilicate glass; frit
Photo by artist

The multiple encasings of the custom cane core in each bead imply a world within a world, within a world.

MALCOM POTEK

Geode Beads, 2007
Each, 1¼ x ¾ inches (3.2 x 1.9 cm) in diameter
Flame worked; mandrel formed; ground; cold polished; soft glass; metal foils; custom cane
Photo by Kara van Wyk

Silver on both the core and the exterior layer of this bead creates a beautiful counterpoint to the transparent blue encasing.

CAROLYN BAUM

Gardiner Geode, 2004
2 x ⅝ inches (5.1 x 1.6 cm)
Lampworked; cut; polished; soda-lime glass; silver foil inclusion
Photo by Randy Fitzgerald

47

Off-Mandrel Galaxy Pendant

Ideal as a lovely centerpiece in a strand of beads, this pendant can also be worn alone as a stunning focal bead. The inclusion of silver-enriched glass lends it the look of a bead made with exotic borosilicate glass.

What Will This Session Teach?

This pendant affords an opportunity to work with asymmetrical shapes—without the steadying benefit of a mandrel. You'll also learn how to apply silver mesh to a bead and how to create a hole in the glass by using a tungsten pick to pierce through it.

GENERAL TOOLS AND MATERIALS

Glass rods:

    Clear, 8 mm in diameter

    Silver-enriched glass, terra

    Clear, 5–6 mm in diameter

Basic tools (page 11)

Rod warmer (optional)

Scissors

Sharp, pointed tweezers

Large, serrated or non-serrated tweezers

SPECIAL TOOLS AND MATERIALS

Spiral bead masher

Fine silver mesh

Tungsten pick

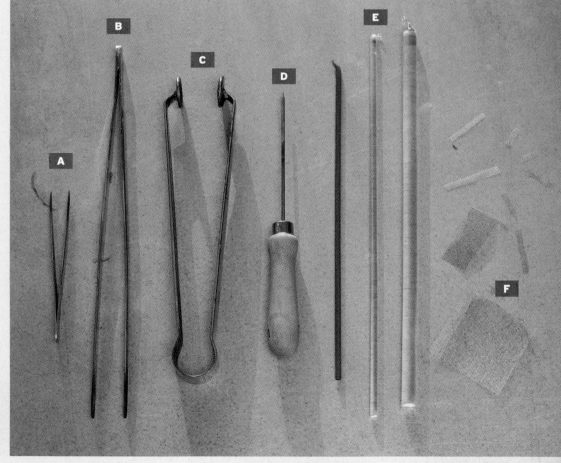

(A) Pointed tweezers,
(B) non-serrated tweezers,
(C) spiral bead masher,
(D) tungsten pick,
(E) glass rods, and
(F) fine silver mesh

Notes on Specialty Tools and Materials

You'll need some special tools and materials to make the Off-Mandrel Galaxy Pendant.

Spiral bead masher: The handheld masher we'll use here leaves a spiral impression, but you're welcome to use another masher if you like.

Fine silver mesh: This material, available from lampwork suppliers and some specialty jewelry-supply companies, comes in small pieces, usually about 2 inches square (5.1 cm). The mesh is easy to cut with scissors. For this pendant, cut it into narrow strips, about ¼ inch (6 mm) wide and 1 to 1½ (2.5 to 3.8 cm) inches long.

Tungsten pick: Purchase a pick with a sharp, pointed tip; you'll need it in order to pierce a hole in the pendant. Over time, the tip will dull, and if you accidentally drop the pick, it can fracture. To resharpen a dull tip, I use a powdered chemical product made specifically for sharpening tungsten; it's available from welders' supply shops. Put on a cartridge-type respirator, heat up the end of the pick, and swirl it around in the jar of powder. In 30 seconds, the reaction between the powder and tungsten will leave your pick with a new, sharp point.

An Overview

The silver-laden glass in this pendant is expensive; to minimize the amount required, the pendant is built on a core of transparent glass. We'll start by encasing a gather of this clear glass with silver-enriched glass, and mashing it into shape at the end of the rod. Then we'll embellish the completed shape with silver mesh and disconnect it from the rod. To make the hole, we'll pierce the glass with a tungsten pick.

Before you begin, preheat one end of the larger clear glass rod in a rod warmer or kiln (photo 1) to make it less prone to thermal shock when it's first exposed to the flame.

Creating the Pendant

Making and Mashing the Bead

Carefully introduce the preheated rod into the flame. Remember to heat its entire circumference in order to avoid fractures. After the rod is warm, create a large gather on the end, approximately ½ inch (1.3 cm) in diameter (photo 2).

Once the gather is no longer molten, encase it with the silver-enriched glass. The method of encasing isn't crucial, but I usually coil the glass in a spiral from the end of the gather closest to the rod up to the tip (photo 3). Be careful to wrap each coil tightly against the previous one so that you don't trap any air bubbles. Gently heat the encased gather until the coils are smoothed. Encasing reactive silver glass will cause attractive and somewhat random variations in its color, so stripe a little clear glass on top of it in a random pattern (photo 4) and melt this clear glass in.

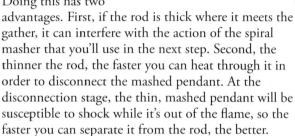

Before mashing the pendant, thin out the glass just above the gather by warming the rod and letting the weight of the gather elongate it (photo 5). Doing this has two advantages. First, if the rod is thick where it meets the gather, it can interfere with the action of the spiral masher that you'll use in the next step. Second, the thinner the rod, the faster you can heat through it in order to disconnect the mashed pendant. At the disconnection stage, the thin, mashed pendant will be susceptible to shock while it's out of the flame, so the faster you can separate it from the rod, the better.

Reheat the gather, keeping it symmetrical; then mash it with the spiral masher or with another masher, if you prefer (photos 6 and 7). After mashing, it's important to keep warming both sides of the pendant, but avoid heating it so much that it loses its shape or becomes deformed.

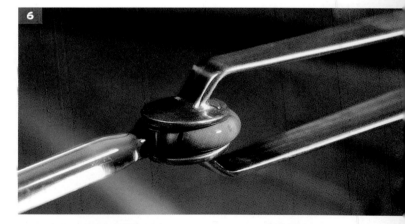

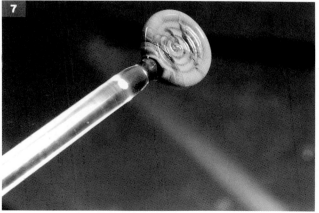

Applying the Fine Silver Mesh

The advantage of using silver mesh with this pendant, rather than silver wire or leaf, is that you can apply plenty of silver to its face by using only a few small pieces of mesh—and a minimum of heat. Heat the reverse side of the pendant, since it will be ignored in the next step. Then heat one edge of the pendant until it just begins to glow. Using pointed tweezers, poke one end of the mesh into the heated glass (photo 8), bend it until it contacts the face, and press it onto the glass as much as possible (photo 9). Heat the mesh and the entire pendant. The

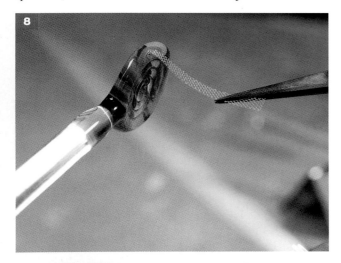

silver will ball up and stick to the glass when it's melted in the flame. Repeat the application elsewhere on the pendant, making sure that the entire pendant remains warm.

It's easier to retain the grid pattern of the mesh when the bead is flat and the mesh is in full contact with its surface, rather than bridging grooves in the glass surface, as the mesh does here. If you'd like to use fine silver wire instead of mesh, just refer to page 42.

Making the Hole

Slightly warm the large tweezers in the back of the flame. Then use them to hold the pendant while you burn through the clear rod to remove it (photo 10). After

flattening the small gather that's left behind on the pendant, you'll make the hole through it. This hole can be oriented in the same plane as the pendant or at right angles to it, depending on how you plan to use the pendant in a jewelry design. Warm the little gather and flatten it to the thickness of the pendant. I hold the bead with tweezers in one hand; in the other hand, I hold a handheld marver so that I can mash the gather between the handheld marver and my torch-mounted marver.

To pierce glass with a tungsten pick, the glass should be warm so that the hot pick won't fracture it, but not molten. Positioning the pendant correctly in relation to the flame is important here, too. Make sure that the spot to be pierced is just behind and slightly below the flame so the pick will move directly through the flame and be glowing hot as it enters the glass.

Heat the pick and when it begins to glow, drive its point into the glass (photo 11). Some beadmakers like to

turn the pick as if it were a screwdriver, but I wiggle it around in the glass so that it will create a hole a little larger than its tip. Once you've pierced through to the other side of the pendant, put the pick down. Don't try to quench it; just let it cool naturally. Frequently, one side of the hole (usually the back) is a little ragged. Use the flame to soften the edges of the hole, but if the hole starts to collapse, use the tungsten pick to keep it open.

Re-warm the pendant. Because this glass has a lot of silver in it, I like to use a reducing flame (less oxygen than normal) for this last heating; I find that this brings more of the silver to the surface. The results vary a lot with different batches of glass; playing with them in the flame to achieve different effects is fun. Now pop the pendant into the kiln.

Further Explorations

LEAF PENDANT

The Leaf Pendant shown here was made with a handheld, leaf-shaped specialty press. I used a 5- to 6-mm clear rod and striped the gather with transparent medium grass green, medium amber, and a small amount of reactive reduction glass. The reduction glass tends to become beige and silver, which works well with the other colors I chose.

After making the clear gather and striping it, I heated it evenly and elongated it slightly by allowing it to droop (photo 12). Then I pressed it with a handheld leaf press (photo 13). I like to play with the pressed leaf to make it

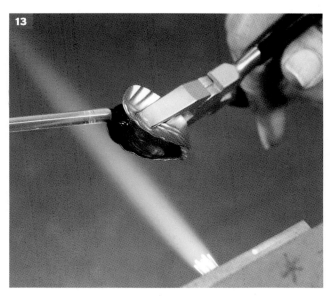

unique; I sometimes melt it, then pull it into a longer shape (photo 14); twist it to curve the body of the leaf; and/or use my knife to carve deeper veins (photo 15).

Then, holding the leaf in pre-warmed tweezers, I disconnected the rod, leaving a small gather behind. I flattened that gather slightly and pierced it with the heated tungsten pick (photo 16). After cleaning up the rough edges around the hole with the heat of the flame, I warmed the entire leaf one more time and popped it into the kiln.

These delicate leaves and flowers were made off-mandrel on wire, instead of on the end of a glass rod.

CAROLYN BAUM

Winter in Florida, 2007
1⅝ x 1⅝ inches (4.1 x 4.1 cm)
Lampworked; layered; soda-lime glass
Photo by Randy Fitzgerald

This lovely rose appears similar to the Rose Bead on page 114, but its off-mandrel creation allows for very different stringing opportunities.

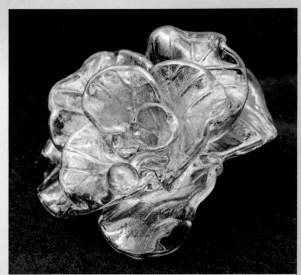

RACHELLE GOLDREICH

Gold-Fumed Rose, 2006
2³⁄₁₆ x 1⅛ inches (5.6 x 2.8 cm)
Fumed; assembled; borosilicate glass
Photo by Robyn Keller Elbaz

LIBBY LEUCHTMAN

Complex, Off-Mandrel Pendants, 2007
Various sizes
Torch worked; formed off-mandrel; acid washed
Photo by Robert Diamante

Several of these captivating focal pendants were created off-mandrel and then attached to glass bails, in the same manner as the Fantasy Flower Pendant on page 119.

The lower portion of this pendant was made off-mandrel and then attached at the torch to the tubular bead.

W. BRAD PEARSON

Lapidary Series, 2006
2½ x 1¾ inches (6.7 x 4.5 cm)
Formed off-mandrel; attached; ground
Photo by artist

These off-mandrel leaves were completed with loops of the rod from which the leaves "grew."

DONNA NOVA

Leaf Waterfall, 2007
18 inches (45.7 cm) from top
Lampworked
Necklace designed by Judy Shapiro
Photo by Titus Paulsel

Blown
Hollow
Bead

*Like many hollow beads,
this beautiful sphere and square are
lightweight and translucent, and afford
countless design opportunities. They can be
worn alone on cables, but also work well
strung with seed beads through their cores
or filled with bits of ephemera.*

What Will This Session Teach?

Typically, a hollow bead is made from two disks built a small distance apart from each other and then either bent or coiled toward each other so that they can be seamed. For this method to be successful, however, the disks must be thin so their weight won't collapse the bead, which rounds and expands when the air trapped inside is heated and expands. The potential pitfall with this method is that thin disks are hard to create; they lose their heat very quickly and tend to be more prone to shock than thick ones.

It's easier to do what we're going to do here—build a hollow bead around the pierced hole in a puffy mandrel and combine traditional torchwork (or lampwork) with glass blowing. The disks you start with don't have to be unusually thin. The bead is wound in the traditional manner, one wrap on top of another, but then it's inflated, using both the traditional method (warming the interior air) and by blowing an extra puff of air into it through the mandrel.

GENERAL TOOLS AND MATERIALS

Glass rods:

    Opaque red

    Transparent dark aquamarine

Basic tools (page 11)

Sharp, pointed tweezers

Barbecue masher (optional)

SPECIAL TOOLS AND MATERIALS

Specialty disk masher and micro mashing tweezers
  (aka stamp tweezers)

Pixie dust in a small, metal trough or heatproof dish

Puffy mandrel

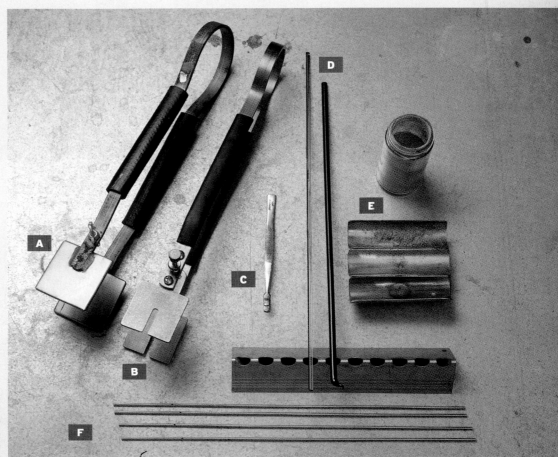

(A) Standard barbeque masher,
(B) specialty disk masher, (C) micro
mashing tweezers, (D) glass rods,
(E) pixie dust in metal trough,
and (F) puffy mandrels

the heat to one spot on the face of the disk and then gently press the disk on the opposite face toward the direction of the heat. The dichotomy here is that you have to warm the disk enough to get it to bend, but you don't want to heat it so much that it begins to collapse. That's why you restrict the heat to one spot. Similarly, you don't want to press the disk in an area that's too cool or press it so hard that it breaks free from the bead release.

Practicing making spacers and disks will make hollow beads much easier to create. When your disks look great to you, you're ready to make hollow beads.

MAKING THE ROUND HOLLOW BEAD (AT LAST)

Wind a spacer bead on each side of the pierced hole in the puffy mandrel, about ¾ inch (1.9 cm) apart (photo 7). These two spacers provide the footprints for the finished hollow bead. If they're a little too wide, now is your chance to use stamp tweezers to thin them a little.

Build the disks on top of these two spacers. I usually alternate adding a wrap to one spacer and then to the other, warming between each addition (photo 8). Any approach to

building these disks will work as long as you keep both disks warm by directing the heat along the mandrel toward the face of each disk, not at its rim (photo 9).

When each disk is about ½ inch (1.3 cm) in diameter, add wraps to bring the disks toward one another until they more or less meet in the middle (photo 10). Remember to keep warming the disks as you work (photo 11). It won't matter if the seaming of the two sides is a little to the right or left of center.

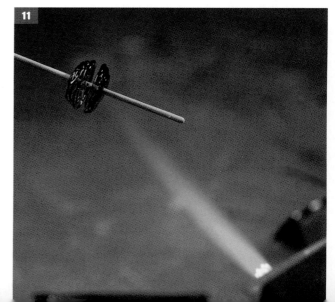

While building this bead, try to make your wraps equal in thickness so the finished bead won't have any fragile thin spots. Also avoid leaving any gaps between the wraps; they'll cause the bead to collapse when you try to inflate it. At this stage, your bead looks no different from a traditional hollow bead although its walls are thicker. It may look a little lumpy and may not be perfectly round (photo 12).

Inflating the Bead

To smooth the coils of glass and inflate the hollow bead, slowly rotate and melt the bead in the flame while keeping your palm or a finger gently over the hole in the undipped end of the mandrel (photo 13). Preventing the warm air from running out the end of the mandrel is important; the bead will collapse if the air escapes. I find it easiest to hold the mandrel in both hands, with my hands to the right of the flame. If you rotate and melt the

bead slowly, any pinholes will be obvious; they'll glow differently and will appear as spots that aren't becoming round. To save the bead, seal the holes with tiny dots of glass.

Even though you're doing everything right, including blocking the open end of the mandrel, the bead will collapse inward a little—don't panic. Heat the bead gently and slowly (don't rush this part); before taking the next step, you must establish an even heat base throughout the bead.

While slowly rotating the mandrel so that the bead stays on center, and keeping the bead parallel to the table, bring the open end of the mandrel up to your mouth and block it by gently pressing the mandrel against your lip or tongue (photo 14). Keeping the bead centered is easy at this stage because you're looking at it down the length of the mandrel (photo 15). Slowly rotate the mandrel until the bead has just lost its glow. (It sometimes helps to wet your lips so the tube slides easily between them.) Next, blow a gentle puff or two of air into the mandrel; then block it again with your lip or tongue. You'll see the bead inflate, but because the glass is still soft enough to inflate, it's also still soft enough to droop off-center, so don't stop rotating it until it's firm. Keep the firm bead warm in the back of the flame so you can admire your results and assess whether or not the bead is finished. You can inflate the bead again if necessary by heating it gently to an even temperature throughout and then introducing another puff or two of air.

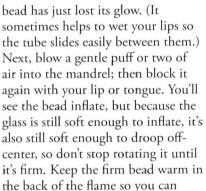

Further Explorations

DECORATING AND SHAPING HOLLOW BEADS

Hollow beads may be decorated with any of the methods used to decorate solid beads, but take care when you melt embellishments into the surface of a hollow; a spot that's too molten may deflate. (Covering the open end of the mandrel and introducing small puffs of air to re-inflate the bead can sometimes be helpful.) Some bead artists blow hollow beads, decorate and encase them, and then inflate them again to give a lovely, diffuse watercolor effect to their interiors.

Hollow beads are shaped in much the same way as round solid beads. A round hollow, for example, can easily be made square by using a barbecue masher (photo 15). (The finished bead is shown at right.) Do keep in mind that the walls of hollow beads are more fragile than those of solid beads; make sure you don't exert too much force when you mash or press them. A hollow bead will no longer be completely hollow if the mandrel contacts it anywhere except at the bead's holes. If the bead's inflated walls touch the mandrel, they'll stick to the bead release.

HOLLOW HEART BEAD

To make a heart-shaped hollow bead similar to the one shown on the next page, start with a slightly wider footprint between the initial spacers (photo 16) and make a fat, barrel-shaped hollow bead (photo 17). Re-warm the entire bead while rotating it; then stop and let it droop slightly so that about two-thirds of the bead is below the mandrel (photo 18). Very gently flatten the bead with a barbecue masher. If the cool metal mashers create dimples in the flat glass surfaces, take a moment to warm those spots and if necessary, puff air into the heart to

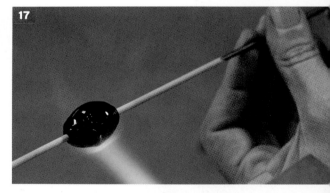

re-expand it (photo 19). Choose locations for the heart lobes on the top one-third of the bead, heat that area of the bead, and form the lobes by creasing the bead with a

desired taper. Disconnect the thread of glass by melting through the connection between the rod and the tip of the heart (photo 22).

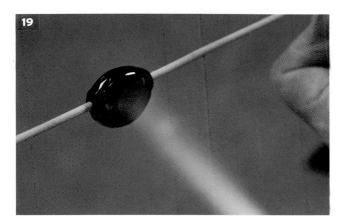

knife or razor tool (photo 20). Gently heat a single lobe; then puff a little air into the mandrel to shape that lobe. Repeat to create the other lobe (photo 21). Finally, warm the bottom two-thirds of the heart, on both sides, until it just begins to glow. Touch the bottom of the heart with a warm rod of the same color and while holding the bead out of the flame, pull down on the tip to stretch it to the

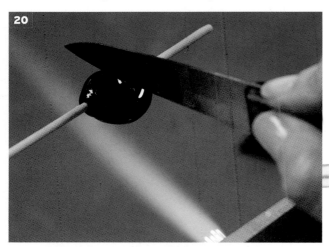

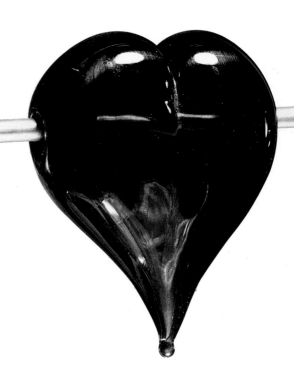

SEASHELL BEAD

Shown at the bottom of this page, this pink-lined ivory shell bead is also lovely when made with ivory glass alone, but ivory is a soupy, opaque color that can be challenging to use by itself. If you choose to make a single-color shell without a contrasting interior color, practice making this bead with a stiffer glass first, or use homemade rods of ivory and transparent medium amber that you've blended together.

Wind two ivory spacer beads onto a puffy mandrel, about 1½ inches (3.8 cm) apart; then roll them into cone-shaped tubes (photo 23). These cones will form the top and bottom of the shell. Starting at the edge of each

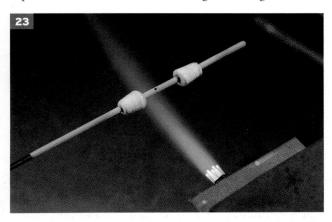

cone that is closer to the center of the bead, add coils of a purple or pink opaque glass to build cup-shaped disks that meet in the middle to form a lemon-shaped—not round—hollow bead (photo 24).

While keeping the open end of the mandrel covered, heat the bead gently to smooth the coils. Next, coat the pink glass in ivory (photo 25) so that the entire bead is a uniform color. If the bead threatens to collapse from the heat of encasing, gently re-inflate it with small puffs of air.

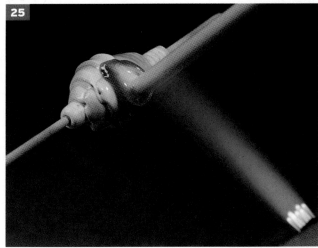

Now, in the bead's center and parallel to the mandrel, heat a strip about 1 inch (2.5 cm) long (photo 26). The heated section will glow, while the rest of the bead remains cooler. Gently blow air into the bead, so that the heated portion expands and nearly pops (photo 27). Bring the expanded bubble back into the flame; the heat will open it up to create an opening in the shell (photo 28).

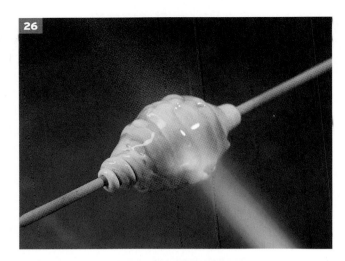

Use wire-bending pliers and a knife to ruffle the edges of this opening (photos 29 and 30). To enhance the shell's spiraled look, use a knife to score a spiral into the top and/or bottom of the bead, on the original tube areas. A shell bead can be embellished with thin lines of transparent amber, as well (photo 31). Adding "barnacles" is also fun; they're made in the same way as the murrini added to the Rune Bead (pages 102–109).

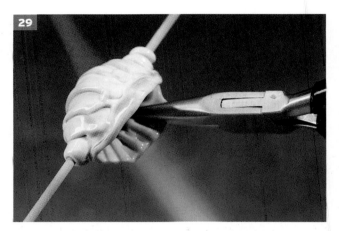

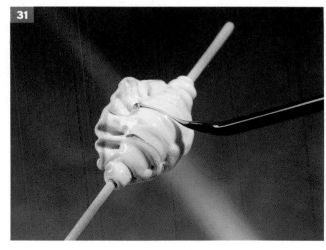

Cleaning Hollow Beads

Clean the interior of a hollow bead where it touched the mandrel just as you would any other bead. I use a cordless, handheld electric drill and a diamond bit, with plenty of water. But what can you do about the remnants of bead release and muddy water that end up inside your hollow bead? The easiest approach is to fill the bead with water and blow it out as if you were blowing out a raw egg. If the bead still isn't clean, the pressurized stream from a dental irrigator will remove the last bits of release. To remove the last of the moisture, create a pad of several layers of paper towels and tap the bead, hole side down, on the pad.

Usually, these steps are sufficient, but in some designs, even the smallest drop of water inside the bead leaves a ring that is obvious—at least to the artist. Another way to try to avoid that ring and eliminate the last droplets of water is to use pressurized air in a can, blown into the bead. If there's no metal at all in the bead's design, wrapping a group of hollow beads loosely in a paper towel and heating them in a microwave oven for 20 to 30 seconds will also work. The beads should get warm, but not hot to the touch.

Hollow beads cry out to be earrings; their translucency and light weight invite an oversized statement.

JILL A. SYMONS

Amethyst Hollows, 2007

¾ inch (1.8 cm)

Lampworked; hollow work; soft glass; Czech glass beads; silver findings

Photo by artist

Because hollow beads are light, they lend themselves to embellishment with many layers of glass, the weight of which would be problematic if made on a solid core.

PATTI CAHILL

Puffy Cubes and Spheres, 2007

Spheres, 1⅜ x 1⅜ x 1½ inches (3.5 x 3.5 x 3.8 cm) in diameter

Cubes, 1⅜ x 1⅜ x 1⅜ inches (3.5 x 3.5 x 3.5 cm)

Hollow work; lampworked; mandrel formed; dotted; raked; plucked; soda-lime glass; handmade millefiori

Photo by artist

*Transparent hollow beads—
the essence of simplicity.*

ANDRÉE KOSAK

Transparent Trio Hollow Beads, 2006
½–¾ inch (1.5–1.7 cm) round
Lampworked; hollow work;
transparent soda-lime glass
Photo by artist

*Creating raised surface dots
requires less heat than melting
dots flush with the surface, so
the process is less likely to cause
the bead to collapse.*

ANDRÉE KOSAK

*Transparent Hollow Beads with
Pressed Dots*, 2006
⅝–¾ inch (1.6–1.8 cm) round
Lampworked; hollow work;
transparent soda-lime glass
Photo by artist

*The restrained application
of enamels allows the
transparency of these beads
to remain apparent.*

BARBARA BECKER SIMON

California Beads, 2000–2007
Largest, 1 x 1 inch (2.5 x 2.5 cm)
Hollow work; soda-lime glass;
enamel; stringer
Photo by Rob Stegmann

Twistie Pendant

Beautiful twisties made from soft glass can be used in any number of exciting ways; these delicate pendants are just one. When I'm not wearing my pendants, I hang them as tiny ornaments in a sunny window. Smaller versions can make great earring dangles.

What Will This Session Teach?

Creating one of these pendants will introduce you to making complex twisties and, in the process, to some challenging off-mandrel work that will stretch your heat-control skills. If the pendant doesn't appeal to you, just try one of the alternatives in Further Explorations (page 76).

GENERAL TOOLS AND MATERIALS

Glass rods:

    Opaque orange (preferably 6 to 7 mm in diameter)

    Opaque olive green

    Opaque medium blue

    Clear, 8 mm in diameter

Aventurine stringer or intense black stringer (optional)

Basic tools (page 11)

Barbecue masher

White glue

Sand-filled can

Rod warmer (optional)

SPECIALTY TOOLS AND MATERIALS

Tubular, stainless-steel chopsticks

Mandrel

Cubic zirconia (or CZs)

Graphite or steel rod (about 3 to 4 mm in diameter)

Fiber blanket

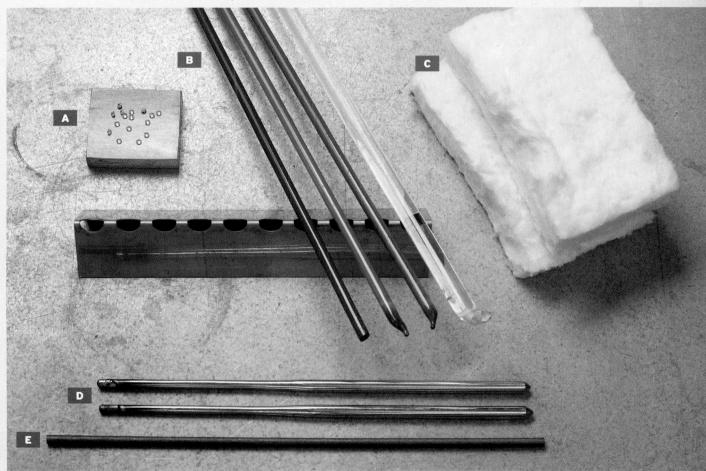

(A) Cubic zirconia, (B) glass rods, (C) fiber blanket, (D) stainless-steel chopsticks, and (E) round graphite rod

Notes on Specialty Tools and Materials

Following are descriptions of the special tools and materials you'll need to make a Twistie Pendant.

Tubular, stainless-steel chopsticks: Used as punties in this session, metal chopsticks have a distinct advantage over punties made of other materials; they won't slump before you're ready to twist. After you use them, quench them in waiting water so that the glass will shock off their ends. Most chopsticks will last through hundreds of uses, but they won't last forever. If you feel or hear gurgling coming from inside a chopstick the next time you use it, set it aside, and when it's cool, throw it out. The gurgling indicates that a hole has allowed moisture to get inside; the chopstick would get much too hot if you heated it again.

Mandrel: A mandrel approximately ³⁄₃₂ inch (2 mm) in diameter also makes a good punty. The main difference between using a mandrel and a chopstick to make a twistie is that the skinny mandrel twists in your hand at a different rate than the larger-diameter chopstick.

Some artists use borosilicate glass rods as punties. These won't soften before the twistie is molten, but the disadvantage to using them is that you have to remove the residual incompatible glass from the ends of the twistie, or the twistie will fracture when you use it with soft glass. I tend not to use boro punties because I'm very cautious about mixing glass types on my workbench; my fear is that I'll accidentally pick up an incompatible rod.

Cubic zirconia (or CZs): CZs, available in a wide array of colors and sizes, are synthetic diamonds. In order to withstand the temperatures of beadmaking, the CZs used in glasswork must be labeled "cast in place." The sizes that can be successfully inserted into glass include 2 mm, 2.5 mm, and 3 mm. Smaller CZs are less likely to crack in a hot bead, so if you plan to encase one in your bead, use a small size; the encasing will magnify it.

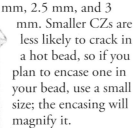

Inserting CZs into a bead can be accomplished in different ways. The easiest method is to place the CZ on a marver, with its pointed end facing

up, spot-heat the area on the bead where you want to insert it, and press the hot spot down onto the CZ. After the CZ is adhered, either gently re-warm that area in the flame so the glass will contract around the CZ and hold it in place, or encase the CZ with a dab of hot glass.

In this session, we'll use a more precise method to add the CZ. Before you start your beadmaking session, use a tiny dab of white glue to adhere the flat surface of the CZ to the flat tip of a mandrel (see the photo at bottom left), and allow it to dry, with the mandrel standing straight up in a can of sand. The mandrel will serve as a great applicator when it's time to insert the CZ into the pendant; when the CZ touches the bead, the white glue will dissolve and disappear, leaving the CZ in the glass.

Graphite or steel rod (about 3 to 4 mm in diameter): Although you can use steel rods to manipulate glass (I used one to shape the hole in this pendant), graphite rods, which are available from many glass suppliers, are somewhat easier to handle because they're lighter and even slower to transmit heat during use. Like all tools, graphite rods shouldn't be used directly in the flame, but they're heat resistant, so you can use them close to the flame.

Fiber blanket: Although this pendant is eventually annealed, as you work on it, you'll cool it by sandwiching it between two pieces of fiber blanket after each stage of the construction process.

An Overview

A complex twistie combines more than two colors. We'll start this one by forming a paddle-shaped piece of glass, coating it with colors, and encasing it in clear glass. Then we'll use stainless-steel chopsticks as punties to shape the paddle into a twistie.

The pendant is made in several stages. We'll cut the twistie to length, add a finial to one leg, and cool the twistie. Then we'll create a setting for the CZ at the opposite end of the twistie, and add the CZ to it. When the twistie is cool, we'll bend it into a ribbon shape, cool it again, and anneal the entire piece. (My thanks go to Pamela Kay Wolfersberger, whose scepter pendants inspired this project.)

Before you begin, pre-warm the end of the 8 mm rod of clear glass by allowing it to sit in a rod warmer or inside the doggie door of a kiln (see photo 1 on page 50).

Creating the Pendant

Forming and Coating the Paddle

Gather up the end of the largest orange rod you have available (photo 1). Tipping the cold end of the rod toward the table will allow you to hang on to the largest possible gather.

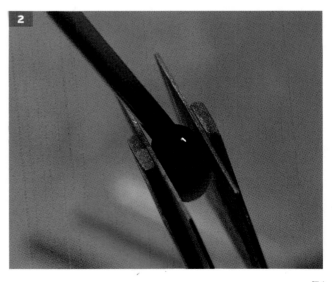

While pointing the hot gather down at right angles to the table so that it elongates slightly, mash it to make it as thin as possible (photo 2). Your goal here is to produce an oval paddle shape at one end of the orange rod. For a longer twistie, just use more glass to create a larger or

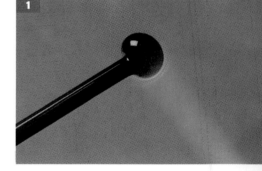

more rectangular paddle. (To make an oval paddle more rectangular, dab a little extra glass onto its corners.) The thin paddle will be prone to thermal shock, so take care to keep it warm in the back regions of the flame while you're preparing for the next step.

As you complete this next step, keep in mind that the visual color proportions in your completed twistie will be the same as the proportions of the colors you use in your initial twistie composition. Vastly different results can be achieved by varying these proportions.

Create a small gather at one end of the olive green rod; then paint the gathered glass onto one flat surface of the paddle (photo 3), covering that surface completely. At

the end of each swipe, use the flame to detach the glass rod from the paddle. On the other flat surface of the paddle, paint a single stripe of medium blue down the center (photo 4). Variations include covering the center of the paddle with color on both sides, or—if you have an aventurine stringer or intense black stringer on hand—adding a stripe of either down the center of one or both surfaces.

Encasing the Paddle

To encase the twistie, we'll use the pre-warmed 8 mm rod of transparent clear glass—a rod roughly twice the usual size.

Cautiously introduce the rod into the flame and begin to create a gather. When heating a rod, start in the coolest part of the flame, with the tip of the rod pointed toward the table so that any glass splinters head in that direction. Roll the rod in your fingers, so that all of its sides are exposed to the flame, and slowly advance the rod toward the torch head. When the end of the rod starts to glow, hold the rod parallel to the table to begin to form the gather.

Because a paddle has two sides, this is a good opportunity to show you two different methods for encasing. On the first side, use the same swiping method that you used to paint color onto the paddle (photo 5). Overlap each swipe slightly onto the shoulder of the

previous swipe, and apply enough pressure to force out any air that might otherwise be trapped between the swipes of glass. Apply the clear glass so that it covers the edges of the paddle. (Leaving the orange edges of the paddle exposed is another possible variation.)

On the other side of the paddle, we'll use the "kiss" method of encasing. Create a large gather on the clear rod. Holding the paddle just below the flame, drip the gather through the flame and onto the paddle (photo 6). To detach the rod, direct the flame at the spot where the gather is attached to the rod, and burn through at that spot (photo 7). The shape left behind will look like the chocolate drop for which this method is named.

Shaping the Twistie

The next goal is to turn the paddle into a fully encased, football- or lemon-shaped construction (photo 8). It's important to avoid trapping air during the encasing

involved in this step. Any trapped bubbles will create air pockets that run the full length of the completed twistie; they'll make it very prone to shock and difficult to work with.

Warm the tip of one chopstick to a dull glow; then direct the heat of the flame at the encased edge of the paddle that's farthest from the rod. When this spot is glowing hot, plunge the chopstick punty into it (photo 9). Move the chopstick up and down, and from side to

side, so that all the colors in the twistie contact it. Then either melt off or cut off the orange rod above the paddle (photo 10). Encase the part of the twistie that is now exposed; then insert the second chopstick in the same manner as the first.

Holding both chopsticks parallel to the table, warm the bundle of

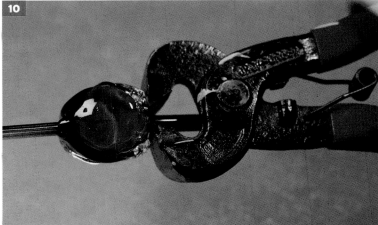

glass by rocking it backward and forward in the flame. Focus the flame first on the right-hand one-third of the bundle and then on the left-hand one-third; doing this will provide enough heat to the middle third (photo 11). Make sure your hands work in tandem; you don't want to add any premature twists to the bundle at this stage. You'll be able to tell when the bundle is heated through

to the middle because the glass will begin to turn transparent. The whole bundle will be quite soupy; if you feel like you're losing control, just raise the bundle above the flame while continuing to rock it toward and away from you. This will allow the bundle to stiffen up a tad and will also keep it from stretching or drooping onto the table.

When the bundle is heated throughout, raise it above the flame and continue to rock it, but *don't* begin to twist until a slight skin appears on the surface of the glass. When that skin is visible, slowly begin to twist the glass, turning one hand away from you and the other toward you (photo 12). When the twistie becomes less droopy, twist as quickly as you possibly can, while pulling your hands away from one another (photo 13).

With plenty of practice, you'll be able to make an ideally shaped twistie—one that's even in diameter (usually about 3 mm) from end to end and that has a smooth surface, without any noticeable grooves in the clear encasing. Using a rod nipper, cut the twistie from the punties (photo 14). This project is perfect for practice; the pendant will look great even if the starting twistie increases in diameter along its length or the surface is a little textured.

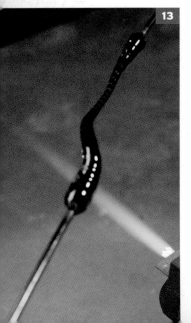

Decorating the Twistie

Cut a length of twistie approximately 5 inches (12.7 cm) long. Slowly warm the tip at one end, holding it at the edge of the flame (photo 15). The goal here is to warm the tip enough so that glass can be added to it without causing thermal shock.

Create a gather at the end of a rod of olive green glass. Still using the edge of the flame, touch the warmed tip of the twistie to the round gather (photo 16); then burn the gather off the rod, giving the rod a little pull as you do to create the pointed finial shape (photo 17). Add a little dot of medium blue to the point of the finial (photo 18).

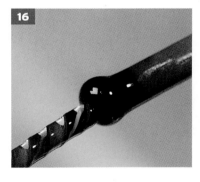

If you'd like to create a finial shape by using a specialty masher (page 76) instead of making the pointed finial, direct the heat at the gather, beyond where it's attached to the twistie, so that it becomes round and symmetrical. Then mash the gather and gently re-warm it to remove any chill marks. Whether you've added a finial or a pressed shape, place the hot end of the twistie between two pieces of fiber blanket afterwards (photo 19). Allow the glass to cool there; don't peek for at least a few hours.

After the twistie is completely cool, it's time to decorate the opposite end. Warm the undecorated tip, just as you warmed the other end. Again, create a gather at the end of the medium blue rod and attach it to the twistie, burning it off in the same way you did the last time. This end will be decorated with a CZ, so flatten it with marvers or a masher (photo 20).

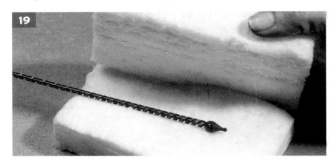

I like to create a bezel by placing a juicy dot of glass where I intend to place the CZ (photo 21). After adding this dot, spot-heat the area where the CZ will be placed, while keeping the entire gather warm. Using the mandrel as an applicator, place the CZ in the pre-heated spot (photo 22). Then

reheat the bezel of glass. Because the heated bezel glass *wants* to be round, it will tuck around the CZ and hold it in place. Tuck the twistie into the fiber blankets again and let it cool.

workshop*wisdom*

Making the Hole in the Pendant

The final step is to create the hole in the twistie pendant. You've already had some practice approaching the flame gingerly with the tip of the twistie; now you're going to approach the flame with its middle 1 inch (2.5 cm). Visually locate this central area of the twistie and introduce it to the bottom edge of the flame. I usually bring the twistie up from underneath the flame, rocking it continuously as though it were a little round bead. Remember not only to rock the twistie, but also to slide it a little to the right and a little to the left so that you're creating stepped-down zones of heat to both sides of the hottest area (photo 23).

When the twistie is soft enough to give under pressure, but not yet soupy, create the loop by bending the twistie as though you were bending the stem of a gooseneck ed lamp (photo 24). If necessary, use a graphite or steel rod to round up the hole in the loop (photo 25). I like to aim for a keyhole shape. Then pop the pendant between the two pieces of fiber blanket to cool for the last time.

When the pendant is entirely cool, place it in a cold kiln and slowly (over the course of about one hour) bring the kiln up to annealing temperature.

Further Explorations

FLOATING HOLLOW PENDANT

This fascinating variation, shown at right, is as amazing as a ship in a bottle; anyone who looks at it will wonder how you managed to get that hollow bead in place.

Make a twistie pendant, with one decorated end and one undecorated end, and create the hole in the middle as we did before, but as you shape the loop, leave the undecorated leg on the long side—about 3½ inches (8.9 cm). You'll find out why in a minute. Now make a hollow bead (pages 56–61), using a ¼-inch-diameter (6 mm) mandrel. Anneal the bead and clean it thoroughly.

While the twistie is still cold, slide the hollow bead onto the undecorated end. Holding the hollow bead as far from the flame as possible (the long twistie leg will allow you to slip the bead quite a long way up and away from the flame), decorate the end of the twistie (photo 26), and then tuck it between the fiber blankets to cool. Anneal the entire pendant when it's at room temperature. If you kept the hollow bead far enough away from the flame, it won't stick to the twistie or crack.

SHAPING AND DECORATING A TWISTIE

Now that you aren't afraid to bend a twistie, there's no end to the possible shapes you can create. The bent leg shown in the twistie below is just one. Remember to keep your fingers away from the flame. Also remember that every time you've introduced the twistie to the heat, it must undergo a controlled cooling between pieces of fiber blanket before you introduce the next bend.

Try creating stacked dots (page 97) at the ends of a twistie or using specialty mashers. (I used one to create the spiral impression on the pendant shown here.)

The flawless execution and application of a simple twistie resulted in this unique and versatile bead.

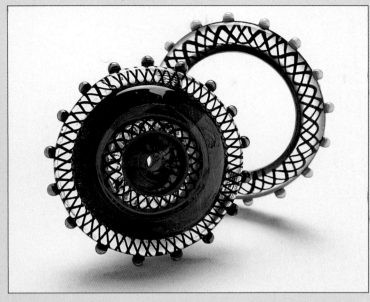

HEATHER TRIMLETT

Which Came First?, 2007

1⅝ inches (4.1 cm) wide

Mandrel formed; hollow formed; soda-lime glass; black and clear latticino and dots

Photo by Melinda Holden

This charming example of a "captive" bead is as fascinating as a ship in a bottle.

JILL A. SYMONS

Spice Cabinet Toggle Bead, 2007

1½ x ⅝ inches (3.8 x 1.6 cm)

Two-part construction process; assembled; soft glass; raku frit

Photo by artist

Attaching twisties to color-coordinated spacer beads transforms them into versatile pendants.

PAMELA WOLFERSBERGER

Glass Scepters, 2006

3½ x ½ x ½ inches (8.9 x 1.3 x 1.3 cm)

Lampworked; soda-lime glass; semiprecious stones; assorted beads and crystals; gold vermeil; silver clasp

Photo by Paul Avis

Hollow Vessel Bead

These lovely vessels, which can be worn as pendants, boast beautiful handles, as well as surfaces decorated with gold leaf. With the addition of mini-corks as stoppers, the vessels can even hold a few drops of your favorite essential oil.

What Will This Session Teach?

The orange Hollow Vessel Bead we'll make here offers a lesson in making *latticino*—or "lace" twisties; one is used as a handle. The appeal of these twisties is that because their cores are transparent rather than solid, the twists are very visible. The vessel is inflated by using a hollow, steel tube mandrel as a miniature blowpipe. Its surface is then enhanced with gold leaf.

GENERAL TOOLS AND MATERIALS

Glass rods:

    Clear, 7 to 8 mm in diameter

    White

    Clear

    Transparent orange

Basic tools (page 11)

Rod warmer (optional)

Sharp, pointed tweezers

Large, non-serrated tweezers

Small dental pick (optional)

SPECIAL TOOLS AND MATERIALS

Hollow steel mandrel (also called a "mini blowpipe")

Gold leaf

Graphite rod

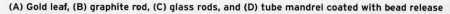

(A) Gold leaf, (B) graphite rod, (C) glass rods, and (D) tube mandrel coated with bead release

Notes on Specialty Tools and Materials

Let's begin by discussing the special tools and materials you'll need for the Hollow Vessel Bead.

Hollow steel mandrel (also called a "mini blowpipe"): To make this vessel bead, I used a ⅛-inch-diameter (3 mm) blowpipe, although a ¼-inch (6 mm) blowpipe will also work. Before using a new blowpipe for the first time, wash it thoroughly to remove any contaminants. Then lightly scrub it with steel wool to roughen the surface so that the bead release will adhere to it more readily.

When you dip the blowpipe in bead release (you'll need to do this before you start making this bead), block the end in your hand with one finger so that less release creeps up inside the tube. Next, blow a puff of air into the tube to blow out any excess release inside. To create a smooth face on the bead release, dab the flat, coated end of the tube gently onto a paper towel. I like to dry my dipped blowpipes by placing them in a wooden stand (photo 1).

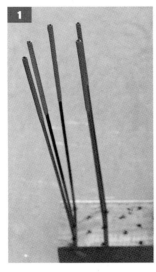

Gold leaf: Use pointed tweezers to carefully remove a piece of a page of gold leaf from its booklet, and place the leaf on a marver. Try not to touch the leaf; it will tend to stick to your fingers and become a useless mess. Instead, tear it into small fragments by using tweezers held in each hand or by holding the leaf in place with a knife tip and pulling away the fragments with tweezers.

Graphite rod: See page 70.

An Overview

First we'll create stringers for the lace-twistie handle. Next, we'll make the twistie. In order to make the hollow vessel, which is a mini-pitcher, we'll create a glass bubble on the end of a blowpipe, and gently expand and shape it. Then we'll decorate the vessel with gold leaf and add the lace-twistie handle that will allow the vessel to be worn as a pendant.

Before you begin, preheat one end of the larger clear glass rod in a rod warmer or kiln (see photo 1 on page 50).

Creating the Bead

Making the Stringers

First, you'll pull a few stringers of white glass, each about 2 mm in diameter. (For this bead, we'll use tweezers to pull the stringers; another method is demonstrated in the Wreath Bead on pages 92–93). Create a large gather of white glass; in order to keep it centered, rock the rod both toward you and away from you. Tipping the cold end of the rod toward the table, so that the gather looks like a mushroom cap on the end of the rod, is also helpful. When the gather is about the size of a fat grape, raise the rod out of the flame, continuing to rock it in order to keep the gather on center and to keep it from drooping onto the table.

In three to five seconds, when you see the gather stiffen slightly (in white glass, you'll also see the color begin to return), grab the gather with your serrated tweezers, at the end farthest from the rod. While continuing to rock both hands in unison, slowly begin to pull the gather (photos 2 and 3). Since we're aiming for a fairly thick stringer, pulling slowly is crucial. Make a few of these stringers before taking the next step.

Shaping the Lace Twistie

Using the smaller clear rod, stripe glass onto the pre-warmed, large clear rod (photo 4) to create four or five evenly spaced, 1-inch-long (2.5 cm) fins around its end. Keep the fins distinct. If necessary, pinch them into shape with non-serrated tweezers (photo 5); their smooth jaws won't make ridges that might later trap air bubbles. (Note that in my haste during photography for this book, I accidentally grabbed a pair of serrated tweezers!)

Now stripe the white stringer between each set of fins (photo 6). Repeat to add a second layer of white stringer on top of the first. Then attach a second rod of clear glass

for use as a punty, making sure that the ends of every fin and every white stringer are touching it (photo 7). Warm the entire bundle of glass, keeping it parallel to the table and rocking it forward and backward in the flame.

Focus the flame first on the right-hand one-third of the bundle and then on the left-hand one-third; this will provide enough heat to the middle of the bundle. Make sure your hands work in tandem so you don't add any premature twists.

When the bundle is heated through to the middle (the white will begin to turn transparent at this stage), raise it above the flame and continue to rock it (photo 8), but *don't* begin to twist until you see the color begin to return just slightly to the white glass. When the color does start to return, begin to twist the glass, quickly turning one hand away from you and one toward you, and gradually moving your hands away from one another (photo 9). Since our plan is to use a short piece of twistie as a vessel handle, a tight twist will look best (photo 10).

Making the Vessel

The method we'll use to build the vessel will echo the one used to create the Blown Hollow Bead (pages 56–61). If you've never made blown vessels or beads before, I recommend that you practice with transparent glass; it's easier to work with because it's slightly stiffer than opaque glass. Also, make a few undecorated vessels before adding the gold leaf, just to get the hang of the vessel shape.

To make the neck of the vessel, wind an orange tube onto the release-coated blowpipe (photo 11). At the top of the neck (the end closest to your hand), add wraps of glass to form the lip of the pitcher (photo 12). Next,

build successive coils of glass, beginning at the bottom of the neck and continuing off the end of the blowpipe (photo 13). These coils will form the body of the vessel, which will be inflated to a slightly larger size. (An over-inflated vessel is extremely fragile; wearing one as jewelry would be impractical.) The key here is to make your coils thick and roughly equal in diameter so the inflated bead won't have any thin spots.

Once the coils are completed and the vessel has acquired its basic shape, warm it to make sure all the coils are fused to each other, and let it collapse onto itself slightly (photo 14). To prevent total collapse, when the

vessel is nearly molten, cover the open end of the blowpipe with your finger or your hand. While rocking the tube to keep the vessel centered, allow the vessel to cool slightly until it has lost its glow; then expand it into a globe shape by blowing a gentle puff of air into the blowpipe (photo 15). Continue to rock the blowpipe as you puff.

Vessels can be shaped with marble molds or other bead-shaping tools. A marble mold is typically made of graphite or a very hard wood such as cherry. The "marble"— or in this case the vessel—is rolled around the rim of a globular-shaped depression in the surface in order to shape it. Other specialty marvers can create bi-cone shapes. I pulled the hot vessel down into a teardrop shape by touching its tip with a warmed rod (photo 16). If you choose this approach, only tug on the bottom of the vessel while the glass is moving in response.

If you tug when the glass is stiff, you run the risk of pulling the vessel right off the blowpipe.

Remember to keep the vessel's neck warm as you work on its body. If you think that the neck might be getting dangerously cool, *don't* rush it back into the hottest part of the flame. Instead, introduce it gingerly into the cooler back portion of the flame to re-warm it. Then walk it into the prime heat of the flame and give it a good re-warming.

Applying the Gold Leaf and Shaping the Lip

Gold leaf is relatively easy to apply. Gently warm the vessel's body; then use tweezers to apply the leaf to its surface (photo 17). Before taking the vessel back into the flame, make sure the leaf is adhered by burnishing it with

a metal tool; the outer surface of the tweezers will work well (photo 18). Return the vessel to the flame and apply gentle heat. You'll see the leaf melt onto the surface and become glossy.

Select a spot on the neck to be the lip of the pitcher. Apply heat to that spot and use the point of a knife or a small dental tool to create a dip in it (photo 19).

Adding the Twistie Handle

Before adding the handle, I sometimes place a glass dot on the blowpipe to serve as a guide, aligning it vertically with the anticipated locations of the handle's two ends (photo 20). Dots like these are especially valuable when you want to position two handles opposite to one another.

After applying some insurance heat to the entire vessel, warm one end of the lace twistie, heat a spot on the vessel's lip that aligns with the dot on the blowpipe, and affix one end of the twistie to that spot (photo 21). This end of the twistie is applied with the body of the vessel just above and to the right of the flame, and the twistie pointing down toward the vessel. After attaching the twistie, flip this arrangement so that the vessel is still

above the flame and the twistie is pointed down at the table. Use the right edge of the flame to soften the twistie (photo 22). Now move the vessel to the left of the flame, with both the twistie and the vessel parallel to the table (photo 23). Attach the twistie to the vessel body in a second spot; then burn through the twistie to detach the remainder (photo 24).

Before shaping the handle, warm the vessel again; it's been neglected for a few moments. I use

a graphite rod or tweezers to shape the handles (photo 25). Warm the entire vessel one more time before placing it in the kiln. The goal is to ensure an even heat base throughout the vessel so it won't crack as it comes to a uniform temperature in the kiln.

Further Explorations

ALTERNATIVE HANDLES—OR NONE

One way to achieve handles of consistent size is to precut pieces of twistie, each about ½-inch (1.3 cm) long. Holding a piece with tweezers, introduce it to the edge of the cooler part of the flame. Preheat the spots where the handle will be applied, and attach the ends of the handle to them (photo 26).

Making handles takes practice, and some beadmakers don't love them enough to invest that kind of time. A vessel without a handle can still be turned into a pendant; just use either of the following techniques. As Jodi Henry has done with her bead on page 89, you can create a lip at the top of the vessel neck, and wrap it with wire later. Or, as the photo below shows, make the vessel on a thin blowpipe; then use a permanent glue—compatible with both glass and metal—to affix a wire to its body, and form a loop in the wire.

LACE TWISTIE WITH A COLORED CORE

To make a lace twistie with a core of color down its center, first warm about 1½ inches (3.8 cm) at one end of two separate clear rods. Then flatten those ends on only one side to make shapes similar to half-round wood molding. On the flat surface of one rod, stripe a bright color (photo 27). Sandwich the two rods with their flat

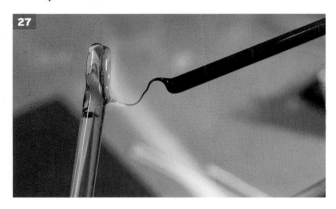

surfaces together (photo 28) and nip off one rod, leaving the section with the colored core attached to the

remaining rod. You now have a fat, solid rod of clear with a color running through its center. Build the lace twistie on the clear exterior; when you twist the cane, the color will run the length of the twistie (photo 29).

HOLLOW VESSELS WITH SHARDS

The lovely hollow vessels shown above and below are decorated with glass shards—thin fragments of a broken glass bubble. The vessel below is embellished with commercial shards, while the shards in the one above were handmade.

Shards are available commercially, usually from suppliers of frit. Keep in mind the importance of glass compatibility; many shards are 94 or 96 COE and can only be used with 104 COE soda-lime glass if they're a very small part of the ultimate design. You can apply shards as a relief, to create a textured surface on a vessel, or melt them right into its surface.

In photo 30, the small jars contain commercial shards, and the dishes are filled with homemade shards, which I'm about to show you how to make. You'll need a ⅜-inch-diameter (1 cm), undipped blowpipe and a large, clean coffee can, paint can, metal bucket, or similar heatproof container.

Using the uncoated blowpipe, create a thick disk of glass about ⅛ inch (3 mm) from the end and about three wraps of glass tall (photo 31). Then create a lemon or tube shape by building successive, thick coils of glass along that first disk (photo 32). (As in the Hollow Vessel

Bead, the shape should extend beyond the open end of the blowpipe.) Be careful to melt the coils completely onto one another so that no gaps exist.

Seal the shape at the far end. Warm it gently; it will collapse slightly but should retain a bubble in its center. Decorate the shape with plenty of color, using frit, many colorful dabs of glass, or a stringer of contrasting color (photo 33). Keep in mind that these colors will become diluted and diffuse after you've expanded this bubble to create the thin walls that will become shards.

Now use moderate (not high) heat to heat the shape gently from the area where it's connected to the blowpipe to the far end. Your goal is to heat the glass enough to be able to expand it by blowing into the blowpipe, but not so much that it becomes molten and collapses. To prevent a premature collapse, block the open end of the blowpipe with your finger or blow an occasional, tiny puff of air into its open end; these steps will keep the warm air from leaking out. Continue to rotate the glass as though it were a hollow bead. When the wraps of glass and all the decorations have fused together and are hot (but not soupy or red hot), slowly blow air into the blowpipe to create an orange- or grapefruit-sized globe (photo 34). Don't worry if the globe is misshapen; the goal is simply to create walls as thin as possible without blowing a hole through them.

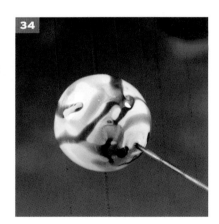

workshop *wisdom*

If a spot on the globe that you blow for a shard is too thin, the globe will pop, and bits of glass as thin as tissue paper will float through the air. These fragments are potentially dangerous if they're inhaled, so if you see a thin wall in your globe, it's better to stop blowing than to let the globe explode.

While the globe is still on the blowpipe, smack it against the interior sides and bottom of the heatproof container so that it fractures, or place it in a bucket and use a tool to break it. Leave the broken pieces in the container until they're cool. Then, while wearing safety glasses, use rod nippers, pliers, or tweezers—*not* your fingers—to break them up into interesting-looking pieces (photo 35). I usually make several batches of patterned shards at one time.

I find it easiest to shock off the hot glass that's still attached to the end of the blowpipe after I've broken the globe into the bucket; I fill another metal container with water for this purpose. Be careful: apparently—although I've never seen this happen—plunging the hot blowpipe into cold water can force steam to travel up it and out the

end that you're holding. You may want to use pliers to break off any remaining glass after the blowpipe is cool, instead.

To apply shards to a vessel or any other bead, first pick one up with tweezers and heat it gently by wafting it through the cool part of the flame. As you do this, keep your vessel warm in the back of the flame. When the shard begins to soften, drape it onto the body of the vessel and heat that area to make sure the shard adheres to the surface (photo 36). Continue to add shards until you're pleased with the appearance. If the vessel gets too hot, it may begin to collapse; just puff a little air into it to re-inflate it to the desired shape. Shards add weight and thickness to vessel walls; if you hope to re-inflate the shape greatly, try to keep the coating of shards even so the overall thickness of the vessel walls stays the same throughout. I like to drape the shards onto the vessel and leave them slightly in relief. Just be sure to flame polish all of the sharp edges if you do this.

The dreamy surface of the silver-laden glass that stars in these beads contrasts beautifully with the silver surface of their highly reduced shards.

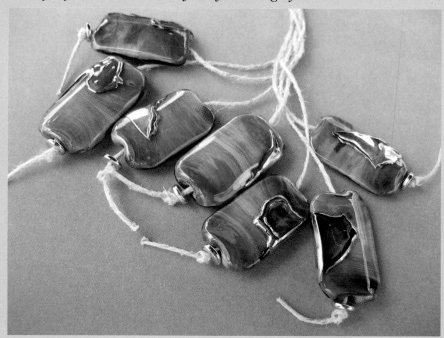

JAYNE LeRETTE

Raku Clackers, 2007
Largest, 1¼ x ¾ x ¼ inches (3.2 x 1.9 x 1 cm)
Encased; lampworked; squeezed; reduction flame; raku; metallic luster shards
Photo by artist

The hole in this vessel runs vertically, so the bead can be wired as a pendant or used in a functional piece such as a fan pull or utensil handle.

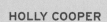

HOLLY COOPER

Phoenix, 2007
1½ inches (3.8 cm)
Lampworked; soda-lime glass; silver leaf; stringer
Photo by artist

The handle of this vessel, which mimics wire or fiber wrapping, is executed in sturdy copper electroplating that is strong enough to support the weight of the suspended, metal-cased vessel.

LAURI COPELAND

Electroformed Vessel, 2006
2¼ x ¾ inches (5.5 x 2 cm)
Electroformed; soda-lime glass; enamels; metal foils
Photo by artist

The wire wrapping on this lovely, handle-free vessel transforms it into a wearable pendant.

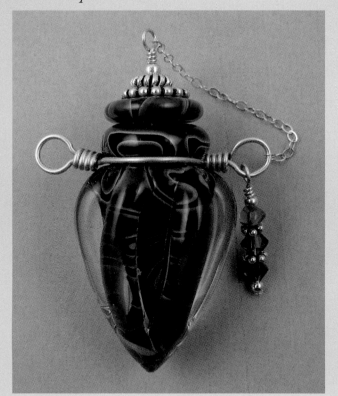

JODI HENRY

Indigo Moon Lampwork Vessel, 2007
2 x 1 inches (5.1 x 2.5 cm)
Lampworked; mandrel core construction; partial raised encasing; soft glass; sterling silver components
Photo by artist

The handles on this hollow vessel were created with spacer beads that were made in advance and garaged in the kiln until needed.

HEATHER TRIMLETT

Roaring Red Vessel, 2005
3½ inches (8.9 cm) in height
Lampworked; hollow formed; latticino and dots; Italian glass
Photo by Melinda Holden

Wreath Bead

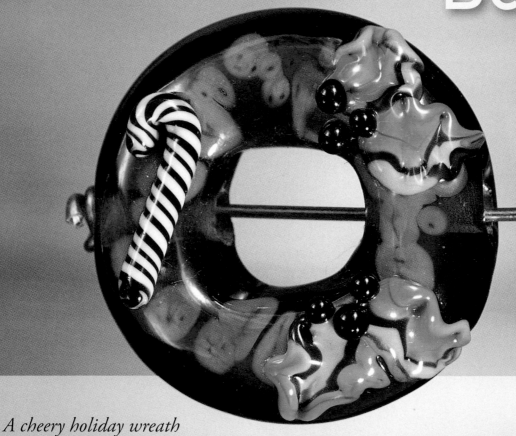

*A cheery holiday wreath
bead looks great by itself on a cable,
but can also make an eye-catching addition to a Christmas-themed
necklace. You may even want to turn it into a stickpin or a small
ornament for special occasions.*

What Will This Session Teach?

This bead offers a great excuse to practice working with a tricky specialty press while we review such skills as pulling a stringer and creating complex canes. We'll also gain experience with the application of a pre-prepared component (the candy cane), as well as with custom-made frit.

GENERAL TOOLS AND MATERIALS

Glass rods:

> Opaque red
>
> Pea green
>
> Light brown
>
> White
>
> Light grass-green
>
> Transparent dark emerald green
>
> Transparent red

Basic tools (page 11)

Sharp, pointed tweezers

Hot plate (optional)

Permanent marker

Torch-mounted marver (optional)

SPECIAL TOOLS AND MATERIALS

Tubular, stainless-steel chopstick

Specialty bead press

Small knife, bead rake, or sharpened mandrel

Frit (olive green frit, medium coarse)

Fiber blanket

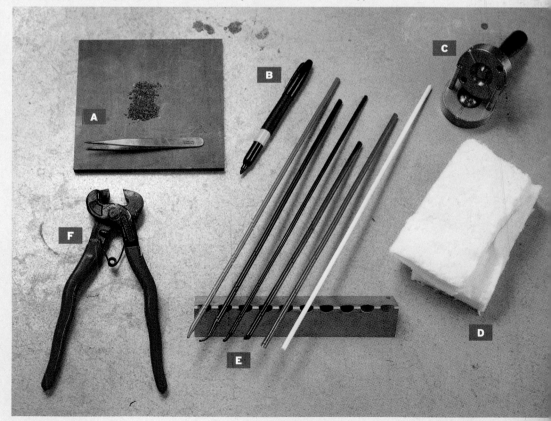

(A) Benchtop marver with pointed tweezers and frit, (B) permanent marker, (C) specialty bead press (doughnut-shaped), (D) fiber blanket, (E) glass rods, and (F) rod nippers

Notes on Specialty Tools and Materials

You'll need the special tools and materials described below to make the Wreath Bead.

Tubular, stainless-steel chopstick: See page 70.

Specialty bead press: Although you can create the wreath shape without one, a specialty press allows you to make multiple shapes that are consistently symmetrical and, in this case, round—something difficult to achieve otherwise. See page 28 for more information on bead presses.

Small knife, bead rake, or sharpened mandrel: As I mentioned in The Basics (page 11), I own a favorite little knife; I use it to shape the holly leaves on this bead. Alternatively, a bead rake with a handle that's comfortable to grip is available commercially. If you don't own either tool, the end of a 3⁄32- or 1⁄8-inch (2.4 or 3.2 mm) mandrel that's been sharpened on a grinding stone will work just fine.

Frit (olive green frit, medium coarse): Crushed glass (or frit) comes in different sizes—or degrees of coarseness—and is available from many different suppliers. (See page 104 for a discussion of reduction frit.) The glass used for commercial frit, which in rod form is often very costly, isn't completely compatible with 104 COE glass, but applying very small amounts of it to a base color, as we're about to do here, expands the available color palette and doesn't compromise the integrity of the bead in the way that mixing large amounts of glasses with different COEs does.

Making frit yourself is easy once you've built a simple glass crusher (see Making and Using a Frit Crusher on page 99). It's an excellent way to make use of little leftover bits of glass and to create custom color combinations. And swapping custom frits with friends is fun. Just beware of combining colors that tend to react to one another, for example, turquoise and ivory; they tend to look muddy and indistinct when they're used together.

Fiber blanket: See page 70.

An Overview

We'll start by preparing the stringers, the complex cane for the leaves, and the candy cane. Then we'll make the doughnut-shaped base bead and embellish it with frit. We'll apply the leaves next, using the complex cane, and then shape the wreath. To complete our wreath, we'll add the tiny berries and candy cane.

Creating the Bead

Pulling the Stringers

We'll use stringers as a component of the twistie that we'll make for the candy cane, to apply the berries, and in the complex cane for the leaves. In the Hollow Vessel Bead (see pages 78–84), we pulled stringer by using a tool; in this session, we'll pull stringer by using two glass rods of the same color.

Introduce two opaque red rods into the flame (I prefer to hold them in the overhand position) and fuse them to one another. Create a gather where the two rods join as they soften in the heat, gently pressing the rods toward each other while feeding more glass into the flame (photo 1). When handling a large gather, remember to

rock it toward you and away from you in order to keep it centered. When your gather is about the size of a fat grape, raise it out of the flame while continuing to rock it to keep it centered and to prevent it from drooping onto the table.

In about three to five seconds, you'll see the gather stiffening slightly and a barely noticeable skin forming on its outside. That's when you slowly begin to pull (photo 2). Because we're looking for fairly thick stringer here—

around 2 to 3 mm in diameter—a slow pull is crucial. As the gather stiffens, speed up the rate of your pull. Detach one end of the stringer from one rod by melting through it with the flame. Holding the remaining rod in your non-dominant hand, rest the stringer on the table. With your other hand, wet a pair of tweezers and touch them to the hot stringer, where it connects to the remaining rod. The water will fracture the stringer and cut it from the rod. After pulling the opaque red stringer, also pull thick stringers of transparent red, pea green, and light brown (photo 3).

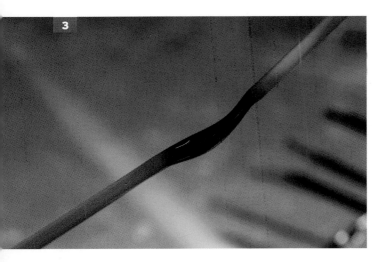

To make the complex cane (or complex stringer) for the leaves, gently warm the end of the light grass-green rod and fold it over onto itself to form a short, fat cylinder. Stripe this cylinder once with the pea-green stringer (photo 4) and once with the light brown stringer (photo 5). Using another rod or a chopstick as a punty, pull a fat stringer about 2 to 3 mm long.

Making the Candy-Cane Twistie

We'll need a tightly twisted, miniature candy cane with as many red and white stripes as possible. Because white glass turns soupy quickly, using white rods as handles for a twistie is difficult, so we'll attach chopstick punties instead. (See pages 70 and 73–74 for more information on chopstick punties.)

Heat about 1 inch (2.5 cm) of the white glass rod and fold it over onto itself to make a short, fat cylinder. Attach a chopstick to the cylinder and nip off the white rod. Now, with the opaque red stringer, apply about four stripes to the cylinder (photo 6). Then attach another chopstick to the other end of the cylinder.

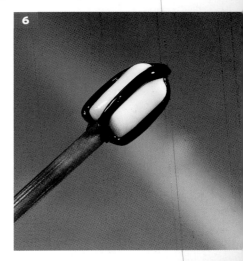

Warm the entire bundle of glass so that the red stringer melts into its surface. Then heat the bundle until it's molten, rocking it to and fro to keep it on center and prevent it from twisting. When the bundle is completely molten, the white will turn clear. Raise the bundle above the flame, still rocking it gently, and begin to twist when the white color is just starting to return to the glass. The goal here is a very tightly twisted cane that is only 1 to 2 mm in diameter, so twist really quickly while slowly separating your hands (photo 7).

After the twistie is cool, gently warm one

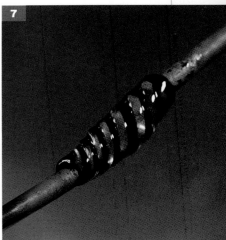

end and use pointed tweezers to form the crook of the cane (photo 8). The radiant heat from the edges of the flame should be plenty to make this bend. Next, tuck the curved end of the twistie between two pieces of fiber blanket to cool (photo 9). After the twistie is cool again, nip the candy cane from it (photo 10), and place the candy cane on a hot plate or the floor of the kiln to keep it warm until it's time to apply it to the wreath. I usually make a few candy canes in advance of making the bead, in case I drop one or have trouble applying it.

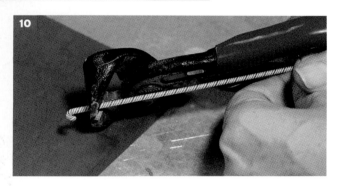

Creating the Wreath

After you've warmed the mandrel's bead release, use the channel in the bead press as a guide to mark the location on the mandrel for the two spacer beads that you'll make to start the wreath (photo 11). The ideal placement for these marks is dead center in the channel of the wreath form. A permanent marker works well; the visible mark will burn off in the flame without leaving a residue.

Wind two transparent dark emerald-green spacer beads at the marks (photo 12). Then, using the same emerald-green rod, begin to build the donut shape by

applying blobs of glass onto opposite sides of each spacer bead. What you're aiming for here is to create two parentheses shapes that will eventually meet at their ends to form a circle (photo 13). I usually find that after I've created a circle using this method, the wreath is a tad anemic; I have to stripe on more glass so that the wreath not only has the right form, but also enough depth (photo 14).

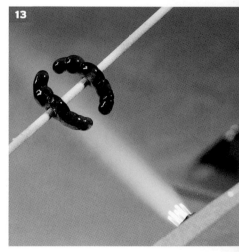

To shape the bead in the press, bring it to a uniform glow, place it in the channel of the press, and slowly lower the top part of the press down onto the hot bead. Be gentle; if you press too aggressively, you may break the bead release. It may take one or two tries at heating and pressing to achieve a satisfactory shape (photo 15).

Pressing cools the bead, so after it's shaped and before you move on to apply the frit, apply some allover insurance heat so that the glass is entirely smooth and the bead is an even temperature throughout.

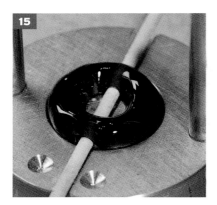

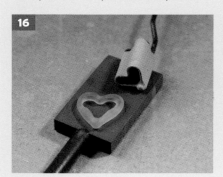
Applying the Frit

Spread a small amount of frit on a heatproof surface such as a graphite marver. In this bead, I used opaque olive green frit that's very close in color to the transparent dark green glass from which the wreath is made; I find that it gives the bead a "tone on tone" mottled appearance. Warm each surface of the bead until it's almost glowing; then press it down onto the frit, one side at a time (photo 17). (If the frit doesn't stick, try again with a slightly hotter bead.) Warm the bead until the frit has melted into the surface. Sometimes re-pressing the bead in order to embed the frit can help, but it's important to avoid breaking the bead release by banging it against the sides of the press.

After you've created the wreath shape, choose a side to be its front. The better choice is frequently the surface with less frit, since the decoration on the front of the wreath will obscure most of the base bead.

Applying the Leaves, Berries, and Candy Cane

To apply each holly-shaped leaf, warm the spot on the bead where you intend to place it; then heat the end of the pre-made leaf cane until it just begins to gather. Apply this gather to the wreath by first pressing it down onto the bead (photo 18), then swiping it off the edge, keeping the glass in contact with the bead's surface (photo 19).

I use my knife to make a crease down the center of the leaf (photo 20); I also carve points along the leaf's sides. To create a pointed leaf tip, heat the tip in the edge of the flame and then, just outside of the flame, touch the heated tip with the still warm leaf cane and pull away the excess glass (photo 21). You can also improve the points on the edges of the leaves this way.

After applying two or more leaves, you'll create the small berries near the leaves by adding small dots with the transparent red stringer (photo 22).

To make the dots for the berries, first create a tiny gather on the end of the stringer. Touch the gather to the bead while holding the stringer and bead out of the flame; then quickly pass the stringer through the flame to disconnect it from the dot. Gently reheat the dots to make sure they're affixed to the bead's surface.

Now pick up the candy cane with the pointed tweezers and gently warm it in the coolest part of the flame (photo 23). The candy cane shouldn't warp or glow; the goal is to warm it, not heat it. While keeping the candy cane warm, heat the spot on the wreath where you intend to apply it. Then, with the bead just above the flame or on a torch-mounted marver, use tweezers to press the warm candy cane down onto the wreath (photo 24). Warm the entire bead one more time, and make sure the candy cane is well connected.

workshop *wisdom*

Whether you're using a stringer to make tiny dots the way we are here, or a full rod to create larger dots such as those in the Dotted Doughnut Bead (page 97), the ideal dot is one that's well attached to the base bead, that has a flat bottom and a domed top, and that sits like a gumdrop on the surface (see photo 27 on page 98). A "bad" dot, on the other hand, looks like a little glass globe or tiny marble on the surface of the bead; it's almost entirely spherical, so very little of its surface is in contact with the bead. You can feel the undercut (or crevice) on a bad dot by inserting your fingernail or a metal tool between the dot and the bead's surface. Bad dots aren't firmly attached and tend to pop off or catch on the wearer's clothes.

workshop *wisdom*

If a surface decoration such as a candy cane or dot pops off after the bead is cool, it's likely that you've made a cold connection. The areas where the decoration and the bead made contact weren't hot enough to ensure that the two were melded.

Further Explorations

DOTTED DOUGHNUT BEAD

The Dotted Doughnut Bead shown here is a silly bead designed to point out the potential of the specialty doughnut shape. The base bead is made in the same way as the base for the Wreath Bead.

Except for the little green tip at the top of each stack, the dots were applied from full rods, not from stringers. (I use stringers only for the teeniest ones.) After the bead is shaped and thoroughly warmed, I create a small gather on the end of the rod, and apply my first dot, holding the bead to the right and slightly beneath the flame (I'm right-handed). Using a mantra taught to me by my teacher Kate Fowle Meleney many years ago, I "touch down, pull away, and burn off in the flame." That is, I touch the rod to the bead (photo 25); pull the rod slightly away from the bead at a right angle to its surface; then bring both hands—the one holding the rod and the one holding the bead— up to the edge of the flame in order to use it as scissors to cut the connection between the rod and bead (photo 26). The force with which you touch down affects the diameter of the dot you leave behind; the distance that you pull the rod from the bead before disconnecting it in the flame affects the volume or bulk of that dot. I re-warm the rod and bead almost every time before I start another dot.

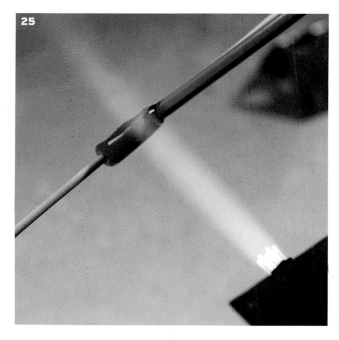

Troubleshooting Dots

To achieve a dot that is well attached to the base bead without any undercuts (photo 27), you'll need some practice. Below are some troubleshooting tips to improve your dotting technique.

27

SYMPTOM	CAUSE	SOLUTION
Dots pop off when you rewarm the bead between dot applications.	It's likely that the bead wasn't warm enough and/ or the dots were very cool.	The bead and dots aren't actually attached to each other because there wasn't enough heat to melt them even slightly into one another. Try working everything a little warmer or bringing the dot into the flame gradually, from a cooler spot, in order to give both the dot and bead surface a chance to warm up.
SYMPTOM	CAUSE	SOLUTION
You have trouble making small dots with a rod.	Either there's too much molten glass at the end of your rod, or you're trying to dot through the heat of the flame instead of next to it.	Warm about ½ inch (1.3 cm) of the rod, and let it cool slightly. Then gather about ¼ inch (6 mm) at the end of the rod to make the dots. Because there's warm glass behind the gather, you'll be able to return the rod to the flame to re-gather the end, but you won't have a huge glob of glass that you can't control. Pay attention to where you're applying the dots, relative to the flame: Are you bringing the bead and dotting rod into the flame (bad), or are you only using the flame to cut the connection between the two (good)?
SYMPTOM	CAUSE	SOLUTION
The bead cracks after you've applied a few dots.	The bead is too cold. Before dotting, warm the bead as much as you can without altering its shape so that you have a heat base that will help warm the bead from the hole outward.	Warm the bead after almost every dot, to bring up its surface temperature. And as you make dots, don't take time to admire your work.

28

Making and Using a Frit Crusher

Start with a 6-inch (15.2 cm) length of 1½-inch-diameter (3.8 cm) black steel pipe, threaded on both ends and capped on one end with a round pipe cap. Cover the other threaded end with duct tape or one of the rubber pipe connectors that are used to connect ends of PVC pipe. (This will protect your hands from the sharp threads.) You'll also need an 8-inch (20.3 cm) length of ¾-inch (1.9 cm) steel pipe (black pipe), threaded and capped on both ends (photo 28).

Place the glass you intend to crush in a dish that will fit in your kiln. I use metal mini-loaf pans from the days when I had time to cook. Put the dish in a cold kiln; then bring the kiln up to about 1000°F (538°C). Using every possible safety precaution—including but not limited to wearing heatproof gloves and safety glasses, using the appropriate tools, and exercising caution—remove the heated pan from the kiln; I use long tongs for this. Dump the hot glass into a waiting container of water; I use an old stockpot—also a relic from my cooking days. Pour off the excess water and dump the now-fractured glass onto several layers of paper towels spread on top of some folded, brown-paper garbage bags. The idea here is to dry the glass.

Please wear a particulate respirator as you make and sort frit; these processes create dust. Scoop up some of the glass (roughly a few heaping tablespoonfuls) and put it into the larger pipe. Insert the smaller pipe into the larger one until it makes contact with the glass, and hammer on the end of the smaller-diameter pipe a few times. Shake up the glass a little; then hammer on the small pipe some more. Depending on what size frit you want, that's all there is to it.

I like to sort the frit at this stage, using sifters that I buy whenever I find what looks like a new size. To make your own sifter, purchase metal screening from a hardware store, cut out the bottom of a paper coffee cup, and tape the screening over the cutout area. I usually separate frit into four categories: useless dust, small, medium, and large. I throw the dust away, but many people use it. If any of the frit is too chunky for my purposes, it just goes back into the crusher and gets hammered again. Empty spice jars make great containers.

The skillfully applied dots on these beads are made even more visually captivating by the vibrant color combinations.

PATTI CAHILL

Puffy Raked Beads, 2007
1¼ x 1½ inches (3.2 x 3.8 cm) in diameter
Hollow work; lampworked; mandrel formed; dotted; raked; soda-lime glass
Photo by artist

The use of complex canes illustrated in these beads requires good heat control; the hollow beads must be warm enough to connect well with the canes, but not so hot that they're at risk of collapse.

ANDRÉE KOSAK

Plum and White Floral Hollow Beads, 2007
⅝–¾ inch (1.6–1.8 cm) round
Lampworked; hollow work; striped stringer; soda-lime and soft glass
Photo by artist

Both the bud and stem on this graceful lily were created with strokes of a complex cane.

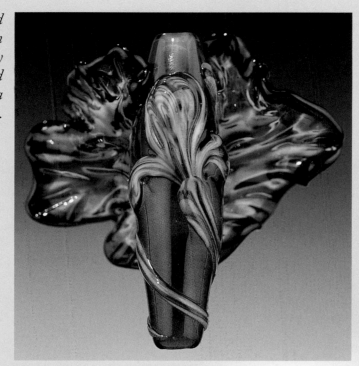

ANN SCHERM BALDWIN

Winged Iris, 2005
1¹⁵⁄₁₆ x 1¾ x 1³⁄₁₆ inches (4.9 x 4.2 x 2.1 cm)
Lampworked; petal and vine cane; ruffled wings; soda-lime glass
Photo by Jerry Anthony

The patterning and shapes on the surface of this bead were created with carefully planned layers of well-placed dots.

W. BRAD PEARSON

Glyph Series Bead, 2007
1¼ x 1 inches (3 x 2.5 cm)
Lampworked; masked
Photo by artist

To enhance the stringing possibilities, a spacer-sized bead was added to the top of this heart, which was created on an open mandrel.

PATTI CAHILL

Ocean Heart, 2006
3 x 3 x ½ inches (7.6 x 7.6 x 1.3 cm)
Lampworked; formed on heart-shaped mandrel; necked; dotted; raked; soda-lime glass
Photo by artist

101

Rune Bead

My interest in communicating thoughts and feelings beyond those already flowing from a bead's actual appearance resulted in this design. The rune in it is the symbol for "good luck." Although the bead is fun to wear, it also makes a great wishing stone to carry in your pocket.

What Will This Session Teach?

This small bead packs a big lesson. As you make it, you'll learn several intermediate skills that are building-block elements for many bead styles: the precise application of stringer, making and applying *murrini* (I'll describe these in a minute), and applying reduction frit. You'll get practice making simple dots and will also work with some interesting tools: the shape of the bead is achieved with a specialty bead press, and a handheld optic mold will help you create the murrini embellishment.

Murrini, simply defined, are slices taken from a bundle of glass that's been fused together and then pulled to a smaller diameter. Each slice yields an image or pattern within its cross section. A complex example might include words. Shown at right, for example, are two murrini slices with my name spelled in them; they were made for me by glass artist Mike Edmondson. A simpler example would be a bull's-eye cane such as the one made for the petals in the Rose Bead (pages 114–119), which would yield murrini with concentric rings.

GENERAL TOOLS AND MATERIALS

Glass rods:

>   Opaque white

>   Intense black

>   Clear

>   Transparent cobalt blue

>   Transparent black

Basic tools (page 11)

Mandrel, 1/16-inch (1.6 mm) in diameter

Large, serrated tweezers

Sharp, pointed tweezers

SPECIAL TOOLS AND MATERIALS

Handheld optic mold

Tubular, stainless-steel chopstick

Specialty bead press

Raku-style (or reduction) frit, small

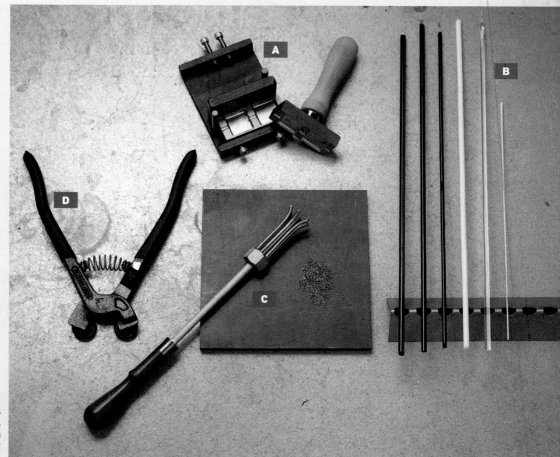

(A) Specialty bead press with base, (B) glass rods, (C) benchtop marver with frit and handheld optic mold, and (D) rod nippers

changes color depending on the type of flame used; it becomes metallic when exposed to a reducing flame (a flame starved for oxygen). Reduction frit also reacts with the base glass to which it's applied, which usually results in a halo effect around each tiny piece of frit.

workshop *wisdom*

It's fitting that the word "rune" has its roots in a Gothic word that means "mystery"; the origins of runes, which extend back more than 2,000 years, are unclear. The symbolic runic alphabet is often associated with the Vikings, but in fact was used by other early Norse peoples as well. Different cultures have used runes as written languages, as magical symbols with specific meanings, and as a means of divination.

An Overview

We'll start by creating stringers of white, intense black, and clear glass. Next, we'll make the murrini with the white stringer and cobalt blue rod. Then we'll make the black base bead and shape it in the press, cover it with frit, and re-press it. We'll set the murrini in one side of the bead (the back), poke clear stringer into its center, and apply blue dots to that side of the bead. On the other side (the front of the bead), we'll use the intense black stringer to apply the rune.

Creating the Bead

Pulling the Stringers
The completed murrini cane will be cobalt blue, with lines of white running its length (photo 1). To construct the cane, we'll need several fat stringers of white glass, each approximately 2 to 3 mm in diameter. To create the rune, we'll need intense black stringers approximately 2 mm in diameter. (Intense black is truly black glass—not

Notes on Specialty Tools and Materials

You'll need the following special tools and materials for the Rune Bead.

Handheld optic mold: A handheld optic mold with steel fingers, which you'll use to make the murrini for this project, is designed for use at the torch and thus lends itself well to beadmaking. Although this mold isn't essential, it makes the job a little easier and creates more precise stripes in the murrini cane. In Further Explorations (page 111), I also describe another type of optic mold.

Tubular, stainless-steel chopstick: See page 70.

Specialty bead press: The base bead for this project is shaped in a brass press that creates square- or tile-shaped beads, but any pressed shape that affords a flat surface for displaying the rune can be attractive. The press we'll use here works best with a ¹⁄₁₆-inch (1.6 mm) mandrel. (See page 28 for more information on presses.)

Raku-style (or reduction) frit, small: (For general information on frit, see page 92.) Raku frit, which is made by several manufacturers, tends to become brown with hints of blues and purples. Because it's reactive, it

the transparent dark purple that is used as black in many instances and in the base bead for this project.) Pull these stringers now; you'll find instructions for different ways to do this on pages 80 and 92–93.

A large clear stringer adds a twist to the murrini in this bead. I like to make this stringer by heating a very small amount on the end of the rod and pulling about 2 inches (5.1 cm) of fat stringer that I leave attached (photo 2). Later, we'll use the rod as a handle.

Each rune requires some strategizing in advance regarding how the design can best be achieved. For this rune, I cut all the pieces of intense black stringer to length ahead of time—except for the central stripe, which is applied from a whole stringer. Photo 3 shows these stringers, as well as the raku frit.

Making the Murrini

Form a gather on the end of the cobalt blue glass by folding over about ¾ inch (1.9 cm) of the rod onto itself and then folding that doubled piece down onto the rod again. The goal here is to make a thick cylinder of glass about the diameter of a ring finger.

While holding the optic mold in your non-dominant hand, heat the cylinder (but not the rod) until it's hot and floppy. Just before you might lose control of it, plunge it into the mold (photo 4) and remove it. (You don't need to push the cylinder all the way to the bottom of the mold, but ideally, you'll manage to get all of it into the mold.)

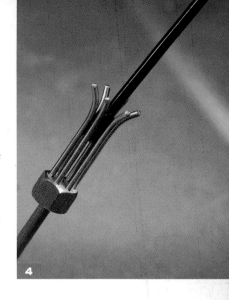

workshop *wisdom*

If you've never used this type of optic mold before, you may find it difficult to balance the heavy glass cylinder at the end of a typical 5 or 6 mm glass rod as you work. One solution is to transfer the cylinder to a metal punty such as a steel chopstick or fat mandrel. The advantage to this approach is that you can get the cylinder very hot without the rod behind it getting soft and floppy.

The cylinder will now have grooves around its outer circumference. Keep the entire cylinder warm by passing it frequently through the flame, but don't allow it to get so hot that the definition of these grooves is lost. Fill each groove with white stringer by attaching the stringer to one end of the cylinder, and, using the radiant heat from just below the flame, pressing the stringer into the groove (photo 5). Pay close attention to the position of your

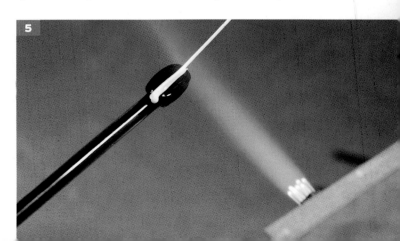

work relative to the flame; as you disconnect the stringer, only the tip of the cylinder should be in the flame (photo 6). After filling all the grooves, take a moment to make

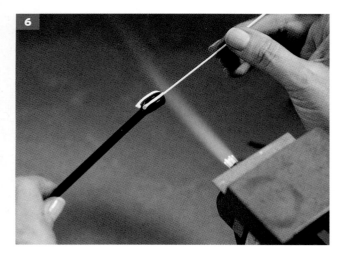

sure that each stringer is anchored at both ends.

Attach a punty (I use a steel chopstick, but a fat mandrel will also work) to the end of the cylinder. Then warm the entire cylinder while rocking it toward and away from you in order to avoid adding a twist to it. When the entire cylinder is molten to the core, raise it above the flame (keep rocking it back and forth), and slowly pull the cane until it's 5 or 6 mm in diameter, or roughly the thickness of a typical rod of Italian soda-lime glass (photo 7). Allow the cane to cool, nip it free from the punty, and cut it into slices about ⅛ inch (3 mm) thick. Even though the Rune Bead requires only one

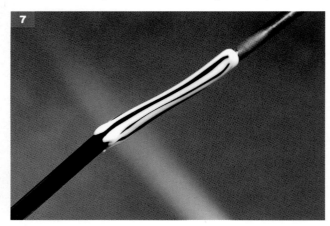

murrini, I like to have a few extra on hand in case I drop one in the course of applying it. To keep them warm, place the murrini on the edge of your torch-mounted marver if you have one, or on a marver near the torch if you don't.

Making the Base Bead

To make the base bead, start by winding black glass onto the ⅟₁₆-inch (1.6 mm) mandrel to form a tube that's about ⅛ inch (3 mm) smaller than the square in the press; you'll press a square from this fat tube. When you're first learning to use a press, getting just the right amount of glass onto the mandrel involves a little trial and error.

Place the tube in the lower portion of the press (photo 8); then lower the upper portion of the press onto it (photo 9). If your tube was too small, and the glass fills the center of the press but not its corners, dot glass onto the four corners of the pressed bead (photo 10), heat it, and press it again. Devote some time to achieving the tile shape of this bead; it won't be reshaped during later stages of creation. Also be sure to fire polish the chill marks from the surfaces of the bead (page 29); you won't be able to do this after you apply the embellishments.

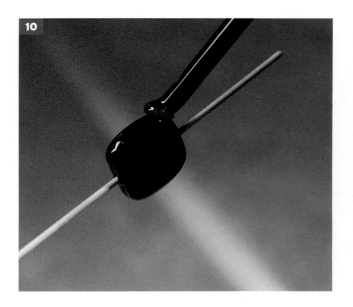

Applying the Frit

Once the bead shape is pleasing to you, it's time to add the frit. I usually apply it from a small metal trough, but for this bead, you should spread it on a flat, heatproof surface instead. I use a square piece of graphite.

Warm one side of the bead until it begins to glow; then press that side into the frit. Repeat this on the other side of the bead (photo 11). The same method can be used to add frit to the edges of the bead, but always be careful to preserve the tile shape. After the bead is satisfactorily covered with frit, heat and gently re-press it to reform a flat surface on each side (photo 12).

Applying the Murrini

Warm the serrated tweezers by wafting them through the coolest part of the flame. Then use them to pick up the murrini, holding it so that one-third is covered by the tweezers and two-thirds extends below the bottom edges of the tweezer jaws. Heat the exposed part of the murrini and the spot on the back of the bead where you want to place it, until that spot glows. Then, with a quick motion and just outside the flame, position the murrini on the bead (photo 13), and use the outer surface of the tweezers to press it securely in place (photo 14).

If you apply heat directly to the flat face of a murrini, it will round up into a ball—an effect that's great for some beads. Here, though, direct the heat around its edges and use a handheld marver to gently flatten it so that it's almost flush with the surface of the bead. Now spot-heat the face of the murrini until it glows. Then—with the bead out of the flame—poke the cold, fat clear stringer into the center of the

murrini (photo 15), giving it a slight twist as you do. Inserting and twisting the stringer will draw the white spokes into the center to create the starburst pattern (photo 16). Pause long enough for the stringer to stiffen in place; you should then be able to snap it off at the surface of the murrini by moving it sharply from side to

side. Re-warm the entire bead, and be sure to add a little heat to the murrini, too, in order to soften any shards of glass left behind by the snapped-off stringer.

Applying the Dots

The murrini is the focal point on this side (the back surface) of the bead, so the cobalt blue dots that trail from it should be small. I apply them using a full rod (photo 17), but if that's a struggle for you, use a skinny rod or a fat stringer. Place the dots randomly, in any way that looks pleasing to you. (For instructions on applying small dots, see page 96.)

Creating the Rune

The most challenging aspect of making this bead is creating the rune with the pre-prepared bits of stringer. The little stringer pieces should rest on your torch-mounted marver so that they're warmed by the radiant heat of the flame. Thoroughly heat the blank front surface of the bead; the stringer won't adhere to it unless both the stringer and the bead's surface are warm. Working next to the flame, swipe the full stringer from the upper left-hand corner down to the lower right-hand corner of the bead, pressing it onto the bead's surface (photo 18). Gently warm the stringer to be sure it adheres, and use pointed tweezers to elongate each end of the stringer to a graceful tip (photo 19).

workshop *wisdom*

A stringer that's well adhered to the surface of a bead will look like half-round molding, with its domed surface facing up and its flat surface affixed to the bead. If the applied stringer looks like a round tube instead, the undercuts (the rounded edges along the underside of the tube) will undermine the strength of the connection between the stringer and bead, and will allow the stringer to pop free.

The two larger pieces of pre-cut stringer that make up the rest of the X shape are applied next. Using pointed tweezers, hold one piece in the back of the flame while pre-heating the surface of the bead. (Be very careful not to melt the portion of the rune that you've already applied.) Apply the stringer piece to the bead, from the center of the stringer you've already applied, out to the bead's corner. Warm the stringer to make sure it's adhered; then pull the tip to a point, as you did before (photo 20). Repeat to add the last piece of the X shape.

The last two pre-cut bits of stringer are added to one leg of the X in the same way that the longer legs themselves were added, but the ends of these small bits are left blunt. Heat the entire bead one more time; it's now ready for the kiln.

Using this stringer-piecing method makes the creation of any rune possible; you just need to plan a strategy for applying the rune's component parts.

Further Explorations

BENT BEAD

At first blush, the Bent Bead (see the photo above) and Rune Bead may not seem to have much in common, but they both offer special opportunities to play with creating unique shapes.

Beads can be curved by using specialty curved mandrels, but may also be bent after they're completed and annealed. One method, taught by beadmaker Leslie Thiel, includes threading heatproof fibers through the cold bead, which is then reheated and curved around a can. Beadmaker Tom Holland has bent beads by using two mandrels to remove a hot bead (one that's no longer on a mandrel) from the kiln; he inserts each mandrel only partway and then heats the bead in the torch to create the curve. I bent the bead shown above by using a curved mandrel and a curved marver developed by bead artist Rocio Bearer. (See her graceful bent bead bracelet on page 113.)

As a general rule of thumb, to ensure that a bead won't be too fragile, its diameter should be three times the diameter of its mandrel. In other words, when you hold the mandrel parallel to your work surface, there should be a mandrel's width of glass above it and another below it. The base bead I make for this Bent Bead is even fatter because it will be pressed flatter during the bending process.

First I create a tube with medium ivory (photo 21). Next, I heat the tube to just short of a red glow and roll it in a double layer of heavy silver leaf, which I burnish onto the surface with a pair of tweezers (photo 22). To avoid prematurely burning off the foil until the leaf is encased in the next step, the bead should be kept in the very coolest part of the flame or below it.

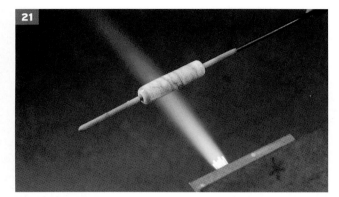

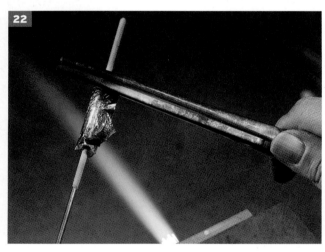

While keeping the bead warm, I create a gather on a transparent medium amethyst rod. I pass this gather through the flame onto the leaf-covered base bead, which is just below the flame, and coil it around the center of the bead (photo 23). Then I add coils of transparent

medium aqua and amethyst to cover most of the bead's surface.

The tricky part now is to press and roll the transparent glass down onto the silver so that the silver is "captured" by it. Because the leaf is heavy and doubled, it will stand up to a fair amount of heat before it begins to burn off. I focus the heat on the transparent glass and force it down onto the base bead with a marver (photo 24). Eventually, as the transparent glass becomes almost flush with the leaf, any uncovered leaf burns off, lending the exposed ivory base bead an organic, earthy appearance. The surface of the bead can now be made smooth (photo 25). I anneal the bead normally, remove it from the mandrel, and clean it thoroughly.

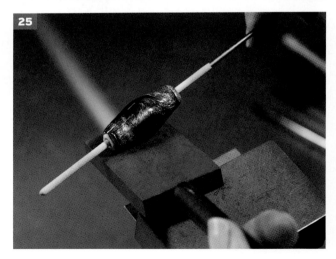

In order to preserve the hole in the bead, 24-gauge nichrome (nickel chromium) wire that's coated with bead release is placed in the bead hole while the bead is cold. I put a slight curve in the wire first—one that approximates the desired curve of the bead. (Curving the wire helps minimize distortion of the bead's hole.) Next, I dip the wire in bead release two or three times, allowing it to dry after each dip. Then I thread the dry and slightly curved wire through the cold bead. (The wire will fit through the hole—and maintain its curve—because its diameter is so much smaller than the diameter of the hole.) Photo 26 shows the wire being dipped, as well as the heatproof gloves, mandrel, and marver that I use when I make this bead.

The curved mandrel I use is made of a combination of cement-like materials designed to withstand high temperatures. I cover it with kiln paper, secure the paper with a twist of nichrome wire, and place the mandrel in the center of the kiln. The cold bead is then placed on top of the paper-covered mandrel, resting perpendicular to the mandrel's length. (Take a look at photo 27. Although it shows the bead after bending, not before, it will help you position the paper, nichrome wire, and bead.)

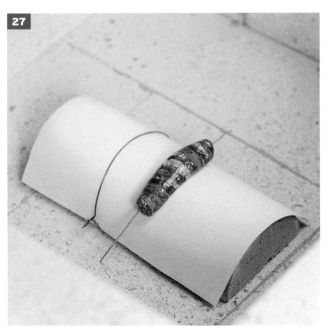

To prepare for the bending, I gather up the specialty marver, heat-resistant gloves, and torch glasses. I then close the kiln and bring it up to 1360°F (738°C). Every kiln is different, but in my experience, bending is easy in the range of 1360°F to 1400°F (738°C to 760°C).

As the kiln nears 1360°F (738°C), I put on my glasses and gloves. When the kiln reaches that temperature, I turn it off, open the lid, and press the marver down gently on top of the bead (photo 28). Experience will teach you just how much pressure to apply in order to bend the bead without mashing it too thin. Next, I close

the kiln, turn it back on, and commence the annealing cycle in the usual manner. I remove the nichrome wire from the cooled bead (it can be reused). Remember to take all appropriate dust precautions in disposing of the powdery residue of kiln paper that's left on the mandrel after firing.

Bent beads make great bracelets and watchbands. I like the way the silver inside the bead fractures under the pressure of being bent.

Optic Molds

An optic mold (typically made of steel or graphite) that rests on a tabletop is an alternative to a handheld optic mold. Both types of mold are used in the same way and leave the same kinds of ridges in the glass. Handheld optic molds come with varying numbers of spikes, resulting in a varying number of grooves. Both kinds of molds are available in different shapes and sizes, so they enable you to make murrini with different patterns and with many layers. One frequent use of optic molds is to shape a bull's-eye or cased cane of several layers; the grooves left behind are then embellished with stringer and sometimes encased again.

Simple murrini are revealed behind a sandblasted and fire-polished window.

DIANA EAST

Decorative Bead, 2001
1¼ inches (3.2 cm) in length
Sandblasted; murrini; enamel
Photo by artist

A starburst murrini is spotlighted by the artful arrangement of contrasting black glass and gold leaf.

JEFF BARBER

Untitled, 2007
1¼ x 1¼ inches (3.3 x 3.3 cm)
Lampworked; murrini; soft glass; gold leaf;
hand-formed sterling silver endcaps
Photo by artist

This piece beautifully illustrates the superb use of curved beads in a bracelet design.

ROCIO BEARER

Spring Dreams, 2006
8 x ½ inches (20.3 x 1.3 cm)
Lampworked; kiln formed; silver glass
Photo by artist

The vibrancy and energy created by the rich color palette of this bead is artistically balanced by a slightly raised starburst murrini.

JEFF BARBER

Untitled, 2007
1¾ x 1¼ x ½ inch (4.5 x 3 x 1.2 cm)
Lampworked; murrini; goldstone; twisted canes; enamel
Photo by artist

The skillful use of stringer, both melted flush and applied in relief, conveys the sense of ancient relics.

HOLLY COOPER

Skylos, 2007
⅞ x 1⅛ inches (2.2 x 2.9 cm)
Lampworked; soda-lime glass; silver leaf; stringer
Photo by artist

113

Rose Bead

A combination of apparent fragility and the true durability of a well-made bead make this floral creation, with its ruffled petals, especially appealing. And once you've mastered its method of construction, you'll be able to create a wide variety of enchanting glass flowers.

What Will This Session Teach?

Making this Rose Bead and the Fantasy Flower Pendant presented as its variation (page 119) will teach you skills that will enable you to mimic virtually any flower. Both beads will allow you to practice heat control—the art of keeping components warm enough not to suffer from thermal shock, but not so hot that they lose their forms. You'll learn how to create cased canes, too (we'll use them to prepare the petals and leaves) and how to assemble a flower on a mandrel. For the Fantasy Flower Pendant, you'll make the bead portion (the tongue-shaped piece that supports the pendant) first, then temporarily garage it in the kiln. The assembly of the flower itself will give you a chance to create a bead without a mandrel and experiment with a variety of tweezers and pliers. The tricky challenge—attaching the prepared bead to the completed flower—comes last.

GENERAL TOOLS AND MATERIALS

Glass rods:

Opaque purple

Transparent medium amethyst

Opaque green

Transparent grass green

Basic tools (page 11)

Large, non-serrated tweezers

Sharp, pointed tweezers

SPECIAL TOOLS AND MATERIALS

Paddle tweezers

Tabletop grill, hot plate, or coffee-cup warmer

Wire-bending pliers

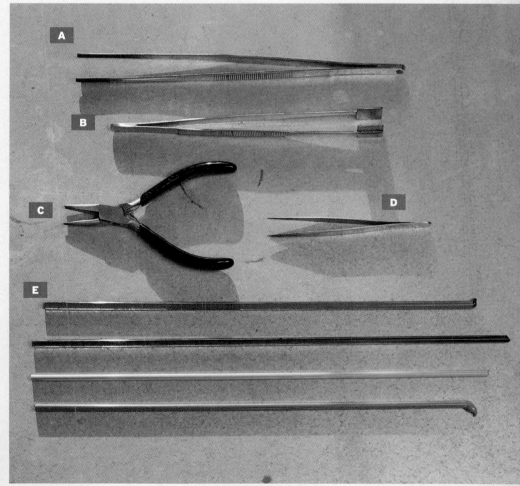

(A) Non-serrated tweezers,
(B) paddle tweezers,
(C) wire-bending pliers,
(D) pointed tweezers,
and (E) glass rods

Notes on Specialty Tools and Materials

Let's begin by discussing the special tools you'll need for the Rose Bead.

Paddle tweezers: My favorite tool for pulling petals is a pair of paddle tweezers. Their metal tips are smooth and are ¾ inch (1.9 cm) square. I use them to simultaneously shape and detach the petals.

Tabletop grill, hot plate, or coffee-cup warmer: In order to keep the prepared petals warm and less susceptible to shock, it's a good idea to store them on a small tabletop grill, hot plate, or coffee-cup warmer. Even better (if you happen to have one; not everyone is this lucky) is a kiln that permits easy access to its interior through a door—and that's *very* close at hand. A kiln across the room won't work; the small petals would lose too much heat on the trip from the kiln back to the torch. At the very least, use a marver or piece of firebrick placed close to your flame; either will provide radiant heat to the glass.

Wire-bending pliers: These pliers come in a variety of sizes and are designed for creating wire loops (photo 1). (Beadmaker Nolly Gelsinger showed me how to use

an assortment of them to create ruffled petals by manipulating the edges of the glass.) They're also used to create the inner circle of petals on the Fantasy Flower Pendant (pages 119–122).

An Overview

The first step we'll take is creating cased canes—one for the petals and one for the leaves. (On page 123, you'll find a description of an alternative—blended canes—as well as a description of another method for making cased canes, known as "swipe encasing.") Next, we'll pull bits of cane into leaves and petals and keep them warm on a tabletop grill. We'll then build the core of the rose on the mandrel, and apply and shape the petals, one at a time. To complete the rose, we'll add the leaves (properly called "sepals").

Creating the Bead

Constructing the Cased Canes

The petals and leaves are both made from cased canes. (The petals are made from a pink core encased in medium amethyst, and the leaves from an opaque green core with a transparent grass green casing.) The benefit of these canes is that you can create virtually endless color combinations by varying the core and encasing colors, or even by adding stripes of a contrasting stringer on the final layer. Pinched leaves and petals made from cased canes tend to have a very pleasing graduated color along their lengths. In my experience, the best result is achieved with a light, opaque core color and a dark transparent overlay.

There are two simple ways to make cased canes. In this session, I use the coiling method, which tends to yield a thicker encasing and therefore a darker result than the swipe-encasing method that I've described on page 123.

Holding the core color in your non-dominant hand, warm about 1½ inches (3.8 cm) at one end of the rod. "Warm" here means the rod shouldn't get close to being floppy and soft, and certainly shouldn't be close to glowing. It should be just hot enough not to crack from shock when you touch it with the molten encasing color.

Holding the encasing color in your dominant hand, warm about 1½ inches (3.8 cm) of it. Then form a gather and touch it down onto the core color, about 1 inch (2.5 cm) from the end. As you do this, position the core rod just below the flame, and run the encasing rod through the flame, at right angles to the core (photo 2). Begin coiling the encasing color around the core. With practice,

you'll learn how to rotate the encasing rod slowly by rolling it clockwise between your fingers as you feed it through the flame; this will keep the entire rod molten as you coil it onto the core. Try very hard to tuck each coil of the encasing color up against the previous coil so that you don't trap any air bubbles. Notice in photo 3 that even though I've angled my hands slightly to the left, the encasing color remains at right angles to the core color.

Continue to coil until the core color is completely encased; then disconnect the rod and smooth the coils with heat (photo 4). If you want a darker and/or fatter cane, disconnect the encasing color, smooth the coils, and wrap another set of coils on top of the first before pulling the cased cane away.

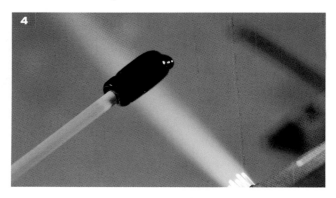

workshop*wisdom*

When they're making cased canes, many students find that the core color becomes floppy as they're encasing it. This can happen if you bring that rod up into the flame (don't), but can also occur when the hot coils transmit heat to the core. Just stop coiling for a moment and let the core stiffen. A torch-mounted marver can be helpful for cooling things down and straightening them out so you can resume casing.

Pulling the Rose Petals and Leaves

Heat the end of the purple cased cane and create a gather just large enough to fit inside the paddle tweezers (photo 5). Then mash the gather with the tweezers and pull it free from the cased cane, cutting the connection with the flame (photo 6). If you find yourself struggling to do this

in a single step, just mash the petal with the paddle tweezers and pull it from the cased cane with non-serrated tweezers.

Place the petal on the tabletop grill or into the kiln to keep it warm. It takes up to 10 petals to make one rose, so pull at least 12 to allow for the petals that are inevitably dropped or cracked. These petals will be more prone to thermal shock than you're probably used to because they're made of two different glasses that have been heated, combined, and cooled, but not yet annealed.

To make each leaf, slightly gather the end of the green cased cane and pinch it with the non-serrated tweezers. Then pull it free from the cane, cutting it in the flame (photo 7). I include up to four on each rose, so I usually prepare at least six. Set them on the hot plate with the petals (photo 8).

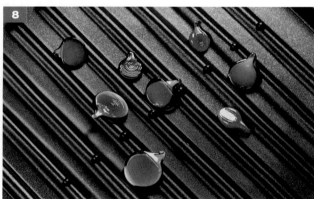

Assembling the Rose

Wrap a small tube bead onto a mandrel, using about one-third opaque green (for the bottom of the rose) and two-thirds opaque purple

(for the top). Add a little extra glass of each color to make the tube thicker in its center, where the green meets the pink (photo 9).

If you take a close look at real roses, you'll begin to realize how many variations there are among the petal shapes. As you apply your glass petals, you can position them close against the base to resemble a bud or curl them back to mimic the unfurled petals of a flower in full bloom. Their edges can be pinched with pointed tweezers, cut with scissors, or creased with a knife. I apply my petals so that the ends that were detached from the cased cane serve as their bases, but you can achieve an entirely different look by rotating them and placing their round ends down on the base so that their outer edges are pointed.

The first round of petals is applied in a ring around the line where the two bead colors meet. Pick up a petal with tweezers that you've pre-warmed by gently wafting them through the back of the flame. While keeping the bead warm on the mandrel, introduce the petal to the coolest part of the flame and move it slowly into the heat. Preheat the spot on the bead where you intend to attach the petal. Also preheat the base of the petal; then press that base onto the bead (photo 10). Shape each petal after you've adhered it (photo 11); once the attached petals begin to overlap, you can tweak them, but you won't be

able to reshape them completely. Attach four or five more petals to complete this ring (photo 12). Then apply the next ring of petals just below the first one, on the green glass.

To create the ruffled edges on each petal, heat the petal edge and use the wire-bending pliers to squeeze it quickly in two or three places (photo 13). Remember to re-warm the rose frequently; the thin petals will lose their heat rapidly. Move around the entire rose, warming, pinching, and adjusting all the petals.

Finally, apply the leaves to the base of the flower in the same way that you attached the petals. On a real rose, the sepals curve away from the petals, but if you're making a wearable bead, I recommend applying them close to the last row of petals, and curving them upward toward the petals so they don't catch on clothing when the bead is worn (photo 14).

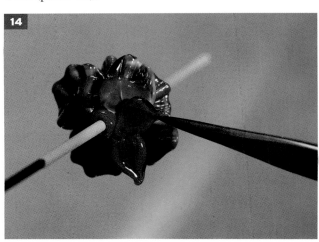

Further Explorations

FANTASY FLOWER PENDANT

Like the Rose Bead, the Fantasy Flower Pendants shown above are constructed from prepared petals that are kept warm until needed. The pendant back mimics the metal bails sold to convert fused-glass pieces into pendants. It consists of a leaf-shaped tongue attached to a small loop and is made of the same glass as the flower petals, in this case a striking orange. (A *striking glass* is one that blooms to its true color after it's been heated, cooled, and then reheated in the flame.) Another interesting effect might result if the back were made to look like a leaf by using a complex cane similar to the one used for the leaves on the Wreath Bead (pages 90–96).

The flowers shown were made with glass rods in striking orange, striking yellow, and transparent medium amber. The pendant back is prepared before the flower and held at the annealing temperature in a kiln.

Start by wrapping a small spacer-sized bead onto the mandrel. Then build the tongue by adding a few juicy dots to one side of the bead and mashing them with non-serrated tweezers. Be sure to flatten one side of the bead so there's a continuous flat surface across the bead and tongue; you'll apply this surface to the back of the pendant (photo 15). To keep it warm, set the bead just inside the kiln, with the mandrel outside so that it will be comfortable to grab later.

The striking orange glass that I used for this pendant tends to "unstrike" slightly when pulled into petals. I like this effect because it provides variegated color. Create a gather at the end of the rod, pinch it with non-serrated tweezers, pull it slightly, and melt it away from the rod (photo 16). The pointed end of the petal, where it was disconnected from the rod, will be its outer edge. Like those in the Rose Bead, these petals can be prone to shock, so I make plenty of them and keep them warm on a tabletop grill or in the kiln. My completed flowers typically have six petals each.

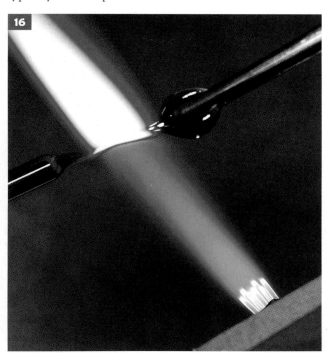

To blush to its true color, striking glass needs the heat of the torch—or in some cases the kiln; the cold rod doesn't represent the final shade. Usually, to strike a color in the flame, the glass should be evenly heated, cooled, and then gently reheated until the color appears. This isn't a universal rule, however; some colors strike in the kiln, so you'll need to learn about the particular glass you're hoping to strike.

To make the disk at the center of the flower, first gather up the end of the striking orange rod, and press the gather down onto a marver to create a flat disk. Then use a button masher to thin the disk slightly and to make it the same thickness around its edges as it is at the center (photo 17). The stainless pads on these mashers are set parallel to each other; one pad extends farther than the other.

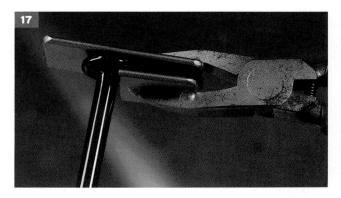

As you take the next steps, keep in mind that the rod attached to this disk is cooler than the disk and petals. Try not to direct the heat onto the rod, or it will crack from shock. Your work on the flower should keep it sufficiently warm.

Apply a ring of striking yellow dots to the face of the disk, keeping them close together and about one-third of the way in from the edge (photo 18). Build them up with

a layer of amber dots, followed by a layer of striking yellow dots. Melt the dots until they begin to slump together; then pinch them with the wire-bending pliers to give them ruffled edges (photo 19). Keep the flower warm in one hand. With the other hand, reheat the end

of the amber rod and create a small point on its tip (photo 20) by rolling it at an angle on the marver. You'll need this pointed rod later on.

Pick up a petal with pointed tweezers. While keeping the disk warm, introduce the petal to the coolest part of the flame and move it slowly into the heat. Preheat both the spot where you intend to attach the petal and the bottom of the petal itself; then attach the petal to the edge of the disk. Repeat this step to attach petals all around the disk (photo 21). (Be mindful of the need to keep the flower warm.) After you've attached all the petals, reshape them with the pointed tweezers (photo 22).

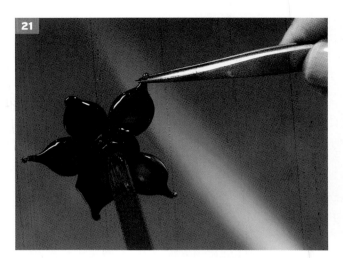

Heat the center of the flower, inside the ruffled ring, and the tip of the amber rod that you prepared previously. Then attach the amber rod to the center of the flower. This rod will now serve as a handle to hold the flower while you remove the first rod and attach the pendant back. Detach the striking orange rod by cutting it with rod nippers (photo 23) or by heating it and pulling it from the flower. Then use the pointed tweezers to remove any rod remnants. *Remember to keep the flower warm.*

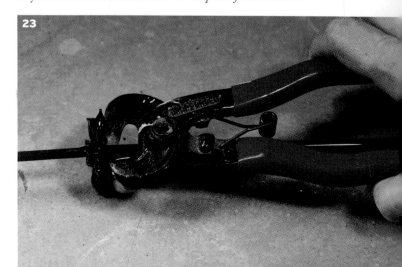

Remove the pendant back from the kiln and introduce it into the cooler part of the flame, slowly moving it toward the torch head. Preheat the back of the flower, and attach the pendant back to it, placing the loop slightly above the edge of the disk (photo 24). I like to position it between two petals.

Now that you've attached the pendant back to the flower, direct the heat at the amber rod on the front of the flower. While holding the flower above the flame and directed down toward the table, disconnect the rod, leaving a thin snake of glass behind (photo 25). Coax this snake into a curved shape with the pointed tweezers so that it looks natural and won't be fragile when the pendant is worn. Heat the flower one more time and pop it into the kiln.

LEAF PENDANT

The Leaf Pendant described on pages 53–54 was made "off mandrel"—or without a mandrel. An alternative is to make a leaf pendant similar to the pendant back for the Fantasy Flower Pendant, but on a larger scale. After making a small spacer bead on a mandrel, add additional glass to one side of the bead until there's enough to melt and shape with a leaf masher (photo 26) or another specialty masher. To make the leaf distinctive, use a kitchen knife to add creases, or create pointed edges with tweezers.

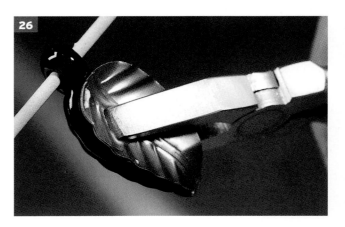

Enamels on Sculptural Flowers

Enamels can be used to vary the color and transparency of the petals on a sculptural flower. (See pages 16–17 for information on the proper precautions to take when working with enamels.) Before pinching the petals from the rod, roll the rod in a dish of enamel and melt the enamel onto it. The finished effect in the pulled petal can be subtle or striking, depending on the color combination of glass and enamel (photo 27). Another way to use enamels is to dip the tip of each warm petal into

enamel after you pull it (photo 28) or after you've assembled the entire flower. You can also sift enamel onto the surface of a flower.

Alternative Backs

In lieu of a pendant back, consider other flat beads that might be used as mountings for flowers. Any tabular shape with one or two mandrel holes will work. Using a T mandrel—a specialty mandrel designed to create a bead with three holes—will allow you to string a flower in a necklace and extend additional strands from it.

Swipe Encasing

Swipe encasing is a method of encasing a base bead, but may also be used to encase a rod. After warming about 2 inches (5.1 cm) of the core color, create a gather on the end of the encasing color. With the core rod below the flame and the encasing gather adjacent to the flame, push the gather onto the core rod near the rod's end; then push it along the warmed inches (photo 29). Using a hot and molten gather, place the next swipe of glass along the edge (or shoulder) of the first swipe. After covering the entire rod, heat it and roll it on the marver to eliminate any ridges left by swiping.

Blended Cane

A pretty alternative to cased cane for flower petals is a blended cane, which is really just a cane made with different colors that are smashed together and only partly blended. Introduce two rods into the flame and overlap about 2 inches (5.1.cm) of each one with the other. As the rods soften, knead them together until you have a pleasing variegated blend (photo 30); then slowly pull that blend into a cane to use for petals (photo 31).

This technique also works for mixing new colors. Just knead the glass until the entire bundle is a uniform color; then pull it into a rod. For flowers, however, I prefer the more organic appearance of petals pulled from rods that have streaked combinations of two colors (photo 32). I also use blended canes to

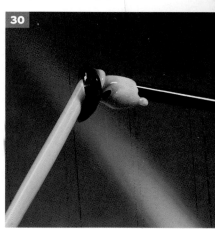

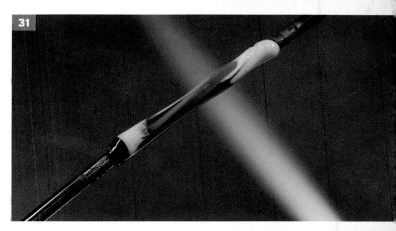

make hollow beads when I want to use very soupy opaque colors, such as ivory. A cane made from two-thirds ivory and one-third amber is much easier to manage when you're making hollows.

Each of these stunning flowers rests on a tabular bead that enables stringing in both bracelet and necklace designs.

SERENA J. A. SMITH

Dahlia Flower Floral Bouquet, 2007
Each, 1¾–2 inches (4.5–5 cm) in diameter
Sculpted; lampworked; soft glass
Photo by artist

These lifelike flowers result from the use of both enamels and complex canes.

PATSY EVINS

Phalaenopsis and Rose Buds, 2007
1½ x 2½ inches (3.8 x 6.4 cm)
Lampworked; sculpted; soda-lime glass; enamels
Photo by Christopher Evins

Careful manipulation of the petals in these flower pendants creates a sense of movement and natural grace.

NOLLY GELSINGER

Pendant Collection, 2007
Largest, 2 x 1⁹⁄₁₆ x ¹³⁄₁₆ inches (4.9 x 4 x 2 cm)
Hand built; dotted; sculpted; glass
Photo by artist

The variegation of color in the petals and leaves creates a wonderful sense of vitality in these glass flowers.

BARBARA SVETLICK

Key's Hibiscus, 2007
Flowers, 1–1½ inches (2.5–3.5 cm)
Leaves, ¾–1 inch (2–2.5 cm) (leaves)
Sculpted; lampworked; soda-lime glass;
seed and miscellaneous beads
Photo by Jerry Anthony

Some of the floral components in this stunning necklace were sculpted in the hot glass; others were created from components.

RACHELLE GOLDREICH

Summer Necklace, 2007
Each yellow flower, 1⁹⁄₁₆ inches (4 cm) in diameter
Butterfly, 1⁹⁄₁₆ x 1¾ inches (4 x 4.5 cm)
Sculpted; soft glass
Photo by artist

Sandblasting

Sandblasting (also called "sandcarving" or "sand engraving") on glass doesn't usually involve any sand or result in anything being blown up! Although sand is used on some surfaces, the abrasive media used to etch, cut, or carve glass surfaces (I describe them in this appendix) last longer and offer finer etched results. "Blasting" refers to how an abrasive is directed at the glass—by means of air pressure. If you search online for information on sandblasting, use "sandcarving," "sand engraving," and "etching" as search terms, too; you'll get good results with them all.

HOW SANDBLASTERS WORK

Sandblasting is executed inside a protective box called a "cabinet." Rubberized gloves that extend into the cabinet allow you to hold your work, as well as a blasting nozzle that directs an abrasive medium at the glass. The gloves are replaceable and come in different sizes. Typically, cabinets are supplied with large gloves that are difficult to use if you have small hands.

The heart of a sandblasting system is the air compressor, which sits outside the cabinet and which delivers the abrasive into the cabinet at a pressure and volume sufficient to force it onto the glass.

While a sandblasting cabinet is in operation, it fills with clouds of dust. To keep that dust from obscuring your vision while you work or floating into the room when you open the cabinet, a vacuum or dust collector is attached to one side. The simplest—although noisiest—choice is an inexpensive workshop vacuum. More expensive and efficient vacuums have HEPA filters. Regardless of the vacuum you choose, abrasive that's been sifted to remove dust and resist particles can be re-used. In-line abrasive separators that filter out non-abrasives and dust are also available.

TYPES OF SANDBLASTERS

For beadwork, either a *siphon blaster* (figure 1) or a *pressure pot blaster* (figure 2) will give great results.

In a siphon blaster, the abrasive sits in the funnel-shaped bottom of the cabinet. One end of a metal tube is buried in the media; a hose is attached to that tube. At the other end of the hose is a trigger nozzle. A second hose extends from the trigger nozzle to the air compressor. When you pull the trigger, the compressed air drags the media up into the hose and nozzle, and through the nozzle onto the glass. Most blasting cabinets come with siphon blasters.

The abrasive in a pressure pot blaster is stored in a pot adjacent to the cabinet and directly connected to the air compressor. The compressed air drives the media inside the pot into a hose attached to the nozzle. High-end pressure pots come with a foot-pedal activator that turns the flow of abrasive on and off. Without that pedal, the flow of a pressure pot is either "on" or "off"; the blaster has no other control mechanism.

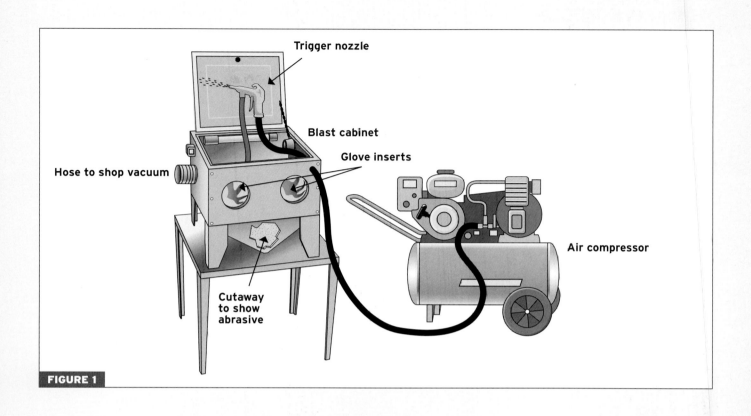

Trigger nozzle

Blast cabinet

Glove inserts

Hose to shop vacuum

Cutaway to show abrasive

Air compressor

FIGURE 1

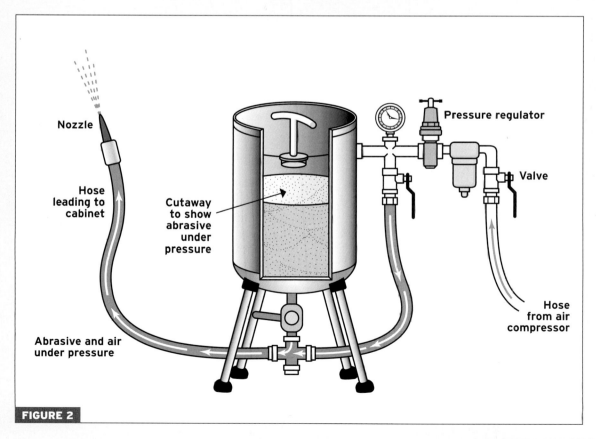

Nozzle

Hose leading to cabinet

Cutaway to show abrasive under pressure

Pressure regulator

Valve

Hose from air compressor

Abrasive and air under pressure

FIGURE 2

SELECTING AN ABRASIVE MEDIA

The two most common abrasive media used to etch glass are aluminum oxide and silicon carbide. Both are sold by the pound and in a range of different grit sizes, which are identified by different numbers; the higher the number, the finer the grit. I prefer grit in the range of 180 to 220.

Aluminum oxide is less expensive than silicon carbide but wears out faster; its grains become rounded and quickly lose their cutting potential. Silicone carbide lasts longer because as it's used, it fractures into smaller grains with sharp edges, which, although finer, continue to cut glass efficiently. Unfortunately silicon carbide's sharp grains are harder on blaster hoses and nozzles, and will wear them out faster.

Never mix abrasive media in your system; use one medium or the other.

SELECTING YOUR EQUIPMENT

Sandblasting equipment varies widely in price and blasting capacity; your decision about what (or whether) to purchase should depend on how much sandblasting you plan to do. One way to get your feet wet is to find a glass shop or friend who will let you rent time on their equipment. Just keep in mind that you shouldn't blast glass with an abrasive that's been used on other materials such as sparkplugs; contaminants picked up by the abrasive may find their way onto your glass.

Always read the specifications and follow the instructions that come with your equipment; the information here is intended only as a general guide. A compressor's air-pressure capacity is measured in pounds per square inch (or psi); its flow is measured in cubic feet per minute (or cfm). Although your blasting cabinet should come with specifications, in order to operate its siphon blaster effectively, the compressor should typically deliver a continuous 90 to 100 psi (621 to 690 kPa), at a minimum of 7 cfm (11.9 cu. m/hr). A six-horsepower compressor is usually necessary to meet these requirements. The compressor for a pressure pot blaster should deliver a continuous 10 to 40 psi (69 to 276 cfm), at a minimum of 5 cfm (8.5 cu. m/hr), and generally requires a two-horsepower compressor.

Although siphon blasters are less expensive than pressure pot blasters, they require a higher volume of air and thus more expensive compressors.

Lower-priced sandblasting systems come with plastic tabletop cabinets; the cabinets for more expensive models are made of metal and are freestanding. The largest cabinets can accommodate large glass pieces and panels the size of entire windows.

In order to see what you're blasting and the results of your work, you'll need a light source inside your cabinet. This can be as simple as a bare light bulb. The top or front of the blasting cabinet is transparent so that you can observe your progress. In better-quality cabinets, this transparent window is protected from the abrasive by a replaceable film.

Depending on the type of compressor available to you, either system may be more affordable. You won't have to add medium as frequently to the siphon blaster, which recycles it from the bottom of the cabinet. When the pot of a pressure pot system is empty, you have to stop blasting and transfer the medium back from the cabinet into the pot. However, a pressure pot delivers a deep etch more quickly than a siphon blaster, which requires a little more time and patience to operate in order to achieve the same results.

Limited use alternatives to sandblasting systems are available, but they can be expensive and frustrating to use. Hobby tools that are essentially cans of pressurized air and abrasive are available, but you can only blast a few beads with one before you have to buy another. And these tools still require closed cabinets. *Pencil blasters* deliver a very small stream of abrasive that can blast glass within a cabinet; they're sometimes used to sign large pieces of art glass. They work well on very small areas, but they're not efficient for sandblasting entire bead surfaces.

SANDBLASTING YOUR BEADS

As with any other dusty process, you must take the steps necessary to avoid creating, inhaling, or spreading dust. I recommend wearing a dual-cartridge respirator, both when you're sandblasting and when you're handling the abrasive. Take care to avoid spreading the dust; clean up with damp towels or with the vacuum system I'll describe in this section.

In order to sandblast a pattern into glass, the parts of the bead that you don't want etched must be protected by a masking material. The sandblasting medium will abrade the uncovered portions of the bead and give them a frosty appearance.

When choosing a resist material, remember that if you plan to blast around the curves of a bead, you'll need to use resist materials with strong adhesive properties. Similarly, if you plan to etch very deeply into the glass, the resist must be capable of withstanding a longer exposure to the abrasive. In the Beach Bead (pages 26–33), where we're sandblasting through tough exposed enamel, we use a vinyl resist that can withstand a long exposure to the abrasive. In the Heart Beads (pages 34–35), however, only the outer layer of each bead is directly sandblasted, so less-resistant metallic paper stickers will do.

If the bead remains on the mandrel on which it was made, before applying the resist, clean and dry the bead, and remove all the bead release from around it. Avoid handling it; oil from your fingers will prevent the resist

material from adhering properly. A bead is always easier to sandblast if it's on a mandrel, so if the bead has been removed, temporarily secure it to a new mandrel with a few wraps of tape placed on either side (photo 1). You can hold a bead that was made off-mandrel in one gloved hand, but be sure to focus the abrasive onto the bead and not onto the glove; the abrasive can cut right through a glove.

With the bead inside the cabinet, the system turned on, the lid latched, your respirator on, and your hands inside the gloves, sandblasting is much like spray painting. Hold the nozzle 4 to 6 inches (10.2 to 15.2 cm)

away from the bead and spray the medium onto its surface perpendicularly, waving the nozzle from side to side as if you were wielding an airbrush. If you move the nozzle closer to the glass, the medium will cut faster, but you run a higher risk of ruining your resist. Moving the nozzle any farther from the glass will slow down the cutting process. If you're a beginner, stop periodically and check to see how your work is going. With practice, you'll develop a feel for how it's progressing, and you won't have to check as often.

If you're new to sandblasting, practice on tabular beads with large flat surfaces. Apply the resist to those surfaces, and avoid patterns that wrap around the edges. Blasting around curves and edges is much more difficult, so save those types of designs until you're more comfortable with the sandblasting process.

As a general rule, although all sandblasted glass looks "frosted," transparent glass gives more pleasing results than opaque glass, which tends to pit and look very dull. Sandblast opaque colors more gingerly and from a greater distance than transparent colors.

After the bead is blasted, wash it thoroughly to remove the resist and any medium. If adhesive residue remains on the surface, clean the bead with a commercial solvent. After the bead is dry, assess whether or not you like its frosted appearance. If you don't, you can treat the etched areas with the vinyl protectant used on dashboards and tires. This product bonds to the glass but can be removed with soap and water.

Sharon prepared this bead for my book before the ink was dry on the contract.

SHARON PETERS

Appendix Waiting to be Taken Out, 2006.
2¾ inches (7 cm)
Lampworked; sculptural techniques; Effetre glass
Photo by Stewart O'Shields

1

Grinding and Polishing

To grind and polish an area on a glass bead, first you cut away its rounded surface and then shine the flat spot (or *facet*) that remains. The high gloss that results is similar to the fire polishing that can be achieved in the flame. Unlike gems, the facets of which are cut at precise, geometrically determined angles and then polished, beads are usually faceted on only a few sides, without the same geometric precision—a process less technically complex but nevertheless time-consuming. Bead artist Lauri Copeland (see her bead on page 47) has reported that her grinding work on a single borosilicate glass bead can take an entire day.

The machine used to accomplish the grinding and polishing processes is a flat lap grinder.

HOW FLAT LAP GRINDERS WORK

A flat lap grinder typically consists of a motor that spins a flat, horizontal wheel to which an abrasive grinding disk has been attached (photo 1). A reservoir lubricates the grinding disk by dispensing water onto it at a controlled rate, one drop at a time. The grinding is accomplished in stages; you start with a coarse grinding disk and work through a series of progressively finer disks; the final stage is polishing the bead.

GRINDING AND POLISHING DISKS

A grinding disk is identified by a grit number. The larger the grit number, the finer the grit on the disk; the smaller the number, the coarser the grit. You'll want to keep 100-, 325-, 600-, and 1200-grit disks—or close equivalents—on hand. If you begin grinding with a 170-grit disk rather than a 100-grit disk, for example, you can complete a first grinding, but it will take longer because the 170-grit disk is finer. You'll start the grinding process with a relatively coarse grit and work with progressively finer grits until your bead is ready to polish.

For the final stage—polishing—I prefer to use optical grade cerium oxide applied with a sponge brush to a felt polishing pad. (Some beadmakers prefer to use a diamond polishing compound.) These products are typically available from the distributors of flat lap units and from companies that sell flamework or lapidary supplies.

SELECTING YOUR EQUIPMENT

There are many flat lap grinders on the market. In order to grind and polish beads, a 6- or 8-inch (15.2 or 20.3 cm) grinder is fine, but larger grinders will work also. (The sizes refer to the diameters of the grinding disks that the grinder will accommodate.)

SAFETY

Always wear eye protection when grinding and polishing. Your bead can become a missile if you lose your grip on it—or shrapnel if it fractures. These dangerous events aren't likely to happen, but there's no reason to shortcut safety where your eyes are concerned.

A flat lap grinder runs on electricity and uses water, so make sure it's plugged into an outlet that's properly grounded. If the instructions for your particular unit differ from any of the instructions that I offer in this section, follow the manufacturer's instructions, not mine.

GRINDING AND POLISHING YOUR BEADS

If you're a beginner, practice on a few reject beads that you don't care about. Until you get the hang of the grinding process, large beads are easier to handle than small ones.

As you make a bead that you plan to grind, keep in mind that the grinding process can increase its fragility; plan on a finished bead that's more than three times the thickness of the diameter of its mandrel.

Once you've made the bead, clean and dry it before grinding. Using a permanent marker to mark the faces that you intend to grind can be helpful (see photo 2).

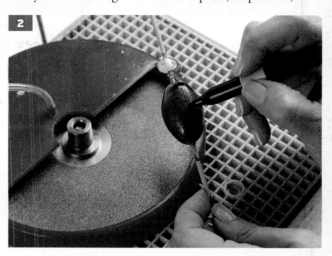

Next, prepare the felt polishing pad that you'll use in the final step. To do this, start by mixing the cerium oxide, following the instructions on the bottle. Then wet the felt pad with water and affix it to the grinder. Turn the grinder on and off quickly to spin off excess water. Using a sponge brush, apply a small amount of cerium oxide to the pad. Three or four brush strokes, made as if you were drawing the spokes on a wheel, should be sufficient (photo 3). The first few times you use the pad,

it might need a little more, but once it's well impregnated, you'll only need to apply more cerium oxide occasionally. Remove the pad and set it aside until the grinding is completed, or allow it to dry overnight.

The first grind is sometimes call "roughing" because it's the stage at which you achieve the *rough cut* (or rough approximation of the desired bead shape). Attach the 100-grit disk to the grinder. Make sure the grinder's reservoir is full of water; then turn on the drip. Each stage of grinding is accomplished with a steady drip of water from this reservoir, so it's important to start the drip before turning on the unit that spins the grinding disk.

Adjust the water flow to a fast, continuous drip; then turn on the flat lap. You'll use the fastest water drip for the coarsest disk and slow the pace of the drip with each successively finer disk. (The polishing process requires little or no water.) If a white powdery residue forms on the bead or on the surface of the grinding disk as you work, the disk is too dry; increase the water flow slightly.

The coarsest grind is completed at the slowest speed—generally about one-half the speed capacity of most units—and the speed is increased slightly as you use finer disks. Polishing is done at the fastest speed—close to the fastest speed capacity of most units.

Hold the bead firmly in two hands and begin to grind the first flat surface on it. Keep the bead parallel to the grinding surface and move it around on that surface in a motion that's approximately circular; don't just leave it on one area of the disk. Stop and check the bead frequently; coarse grinding can happen very quickly. You can always remove more material from a bead, but if you remove too much, the bead will be likely to crack. To achieve a flat surface, do your best to maintain equal pressure on all parts of the bead (photo 4).

After you've ground the initial shapes of the facets, turn off the flat lap and switch to the 325-grit disk. Always rinse the bead, the grinding disk, and the splatter shield on the lap grinder thoroughly after each stage of grinding so that you don't contaminate the next disk with residue from the previous one.

Make sure there's plenty of water in the reservoir, restart the drip (it should be a little slower this time), and then restart the flat lap, setting the speed a little faster

than the speed of the rough cut. This is your last chance to significantly affect the shape of the bead, so grind the facets again. I like to rotate the bead horizontally while I move it in a circular pattern; this helps me achieve an evenly ground surface. The 325-grit disk will grind more slowly than the 100-grit disk and should grind out any deep scratches left by that disk.

The coarser the grit you start with, the more work will be required to remove the scratches left by that first disk. If you're struggling with scratches, begin your rough grinding with a 170-grit disk instead of a 100-grit disk. It will take a little longer to make the initial cut, but the bead will be left with fewer scratches.

Move on to the 600-grit disk. This stage is sometimes called "buffing" or "smoothing." With its decreased water flow and increased motor speed, this step should leave the rinsed and air-dried bead with finely frosted, satiny surfaces and without any pits. During air drying, if you see any bead areas that are drying more slowly than others, they may be due to scratches or pits that have collected water. Try buffing the bead a little more to achieve even surfaces. If that doesn't work, back up to the 325-grit disk to remove the scratches; then buff again.

During the last grinding stage, sometimes called "pre-polishing" or "fine buffing," a 1200-grit disk removes the satin finish from the previous step and replaces it with a very smooth, hazy surface that is almost shiny. If you see any scratches after this step, return to the 325-grit disk.

To polish the facets on the bead, replace the grinding disk with the prepared felt pad. Use little or no water while polishing. The bead will feel a little sticky as you touch it to the wheel; hang on to it tightly, or the wheel will fling it across the room. Don't exert a lot of downward pressure on it as you polish, however; a light touch is called for here. To avoid the risk of heat fractures caused by prolonged friction, polish the bead briefly, and then check your work and rinse it before resuming. Frequent rinsing helps prevent fractures by reducing the likelihood that the bead will overheat.

If the cerium oxide cakes up on the face of the bead, rinse the bead, check its appearance, and resume polishing while the bead is still wet; doing so should add enough water to the polishing process. As you may have guessed, if you see any scratches, you'll have to back up at least as far as the 325-grit disk stage to remove them, and then work back up through the disks to get to the polishing step again.

Near Misses

Sometimes my students complain to me that my class demonstrations "make it look too easy," so I try to show them my beads—warts and all. I thought you might like to see some of the unfortunate beads that gallantly gave their lives to the process of making this book; they're what I call my "near misses." Basically, they're beads that just didn't measure up. I love them anyway; creating them was a tremendous learning experience for me as a teacher and as a beadmaker.

TECHNICAL NEAR MISSES

1 This twisty pendant broke when I let it cool on my table instead of between pieces of fiber blanket.

2 and **3** The upper galaxy pendant broke even though I used fiber blanket to cool it, and the lower pendant is lopsided.

4 The rune bead on the mandrel broke when I held it out of the flame at the perfect angle for a photo—for much too long.

5 The silver-stringer rune bead resulted from my having picked up the wrong glass; I accidentally made the stringer out of reduction glass.

6, **7**, and **8** The geode beads cracked while I was grinding them. (Patience is a virtue that this process requires; so is cooling the bead with water.)

9 and **10** I forgot that these two bent beads were in the kiln, so they sat at too high a bending temperature for much too long. (I've adjusted the Bent Bead instructions, but I kind of like the polished cracks in these rejects.)

11 The petals on the flower are too small and not well anchored on the bead.

12 The hole in the leaf is crooked and sharp.

13 I sandblasted away the head of the poor dragonfly on this square bead.

EXECUTION NEAR MISSES

14 This wreath bead looks silly with berries but no leaves.

15, **16**, **17**, and **18** I wasn't happy with the shapes of the off-mandrel leaf or the three vessel beads.

19 This early version of the beach bead had very oddly shaped waves and clouds.

20 and **21** Poor shaping was an issue with the two flowers. I also decided that the center hole wasn't ideal for the orange flower.

22 This bent bead ended up with slit-shaped holes at both ends—a big obstacle to stringing.

23 This diamond-shaped bead was an early effort to alter the wreath bead shape. I like the diamond, but not the muddy colors I chose.

24 The polished donut looked great, but it ended up being so large and heavy that it would only work as a suncatcher, not as a bead. It's now hanging in a friend's window.

AESTHETIC NEAR MISSES

25, **26**, and **27** The shapes of these vessels and the types of shards I applied to their bodies didn't please me. (I have a small bucket filled with experimental vessels.)

28 and **29** The leaf and wreath aren't quite the shapes I was striving for. They're good beads perhaps, but they didn't match my mental images. I think the addition of the candy cane was a great improvement on the final wreath bead.

30 This beach bead is almost fully actualized, but since when do clouds have sharp edges?

31 This version of the geode bead never made it to print. It wasn't visually interesting to me without some copper treasures buried inside, but several friends like it better than my final version. (Oh well.)

If the process of beadmaking looks easy, it's only because I practice a lot before unveiling a bead to the public. And even with practice, mistakes are a part of the beadmaking process. I'll leave you with the photo below, which was taken during my first attempt to nip the glass rod from one of my flowers.

Acknowledgments

My work benefits continuously from interactions with other beadmaking teachers and feedback from my students. I also rely on the abundant information available from the International Society of Glass Beadmakers, and on the Web. In addition, I am grateful to the following people, who helped bring this book to fruition:

- The artists of the beadmaking community, especially those who so generously provided images of their work for inclusion in this book
- Beadmakers Ann Scherm Baldwin, Wendy Fowler, Kathy Johnson, and John Winter for their shared knowledge and kind support during each phase of this project
- Gifted artists Ronnie Lambrou, Lisa Suss, Suzanne Hye, Judy Ungar, and my mom, Lorry Warhaftig, who provided creative guidance and inspiration for the workshop beads and/or the text
- The entire Lark staff, including acquisitions editor Marthe LeVan, who first broached this book concept with me; senior editor Valerie Shrader, who kept me on track; Steve Mann and Stewart O'Shields, who took outstanding photos; art director Kristi Pfeffer and production assistant Jeff Hamilton; assistant editor Nathalie Mornu; and editorial assistants Amanda Carestio and Dawn Dillingham.
- Freelance editor Chris Rich, who saw me through every line
- Craig Milliron, Lori Riley, the crew at Arrow Springs, and the CattWalk folks, for their technical and moral support
- My colleagues and friends at my day job, who good-naturedly put up with my babble about beads, and most of whom still can't believe how I choose to spend my free time
- All my dear friends, who are my cheerleaders—and who may see a little more of me now that this project has been completed
- My very dear friend and colleague Paul R. Kenny, who is sorely missed
- And most importantly, the following members of my family: Caren Warhaftig, who is a part of me; my nutty and creative sisters, Susan and Linda; my mother, Lorry, and grandmother Sarah; Leah Holland; and the remarkable men in my life—my husband and creative collaborator, Neil Fabricant, and our sons Noah, Seth, and Jonah, who are my greatest blessings.

About the Author

Jeri L. Warhaftig is a lifelong resident of West Orange, New Jersey. She and her husband, Neil Fabricant, have been married for more than 30 years and are the parents of three grown sons and one adopted dog. While practicing law full time, Jeri has devoted her entire artistic life to handcrafts. Her inspiration comes from her mother, Lorry Warhaftig, a lifelong artist in many media and an accomplished painter.

Since 1995 Jeri has set aside most artistic pursuits in favor of a sharp focus on lampworking as it pertains to creating glass beads. Jeri serves on the Education Committee of the International Society of Glass Beadmakers (ISGB) and spends a great deal of time teaching lampworking and writing for bead publications. She has taught both in the United States and in Israel. Jeri exhibits and sells her work at major bead shows and through her website, www.jeribeads.com. Alone, and in collaborative work with jewelry designer Ronnie Lambrou, her beads have appeared in *Lapidary Journal*, *Step by Step Beads*, and *Bead Unique*. Jeri has participated in several juried shows sponsored by the ISGB, in the New Jersey Arts Annual: Crafts (at the Newark Museum), and in a collaborative show co-sponsored by the ISGB with The American Association of Woodturners. Her most recent work seeks to push the boundaries of glass beads through the use of metal inclusions and surface treatments such as enamels. Many of Jeri's beads are sandblasted or faceted in evolving collaborative projects with her husband, "Dr. Fab."

Contributing Artists

Unless otherwise credited, the beads shown in this book were created by the author.

Baldwin, Ann Scherm
Virginia Beach, Virginia
Page 101

Barber, Jeff
Sauk Rapids, Minnesota
Pages 112 and 113

Baum, Carolyn
Gardiner, New York
Pages 47 and 54

Bearer, Rocio
Cocoa, Florida
Page 113

Cahill, Patti
Mars Hill, North Carolina
Pages 66, 100, and 101

Cooper, Holly
Austin, Texas
Pages 88 and 113

Copeland, Lauri
Overland Park, Kansas
Pages 47 and 89

East, Diana
Enderby, Leicester, England
Pages 37 and 112

Evins, Patsy
Hallettsville, Texas
Page 124

Fabricant, Neil
West Orange, New Jersey
Pages 25 and 36

Fairbanks, Leah
Ashland, Oregon
Page 46

Gelsinger, Nolly
Westminster, Maryland
Page 124

Goldreich, Rachelle
Moshav, Michmoret, Israel
Pages 54 and 125

Heilman, Bronwen
Tucson, Arizona
Page 36

Henry, Jodi
Prescott, Arizona
Page 89

Kosak, Andrée
Athens, Georgia
Pages 67 and 100

LeRette, Jayne
Kenosha, Wisconsin
Pages 24 and 88

Leuchtman, Libby
Fenton, Missouri
Page 55

Mehaffey, Louise
Wyomissing, Pennsylvania
Page 46

Nova, Donna
Santa Fe, New Mexico
Page 55

Pearson, W. Brad
Richmond, Virginia
Pages 55 and 101

Peters, Sharon
Oakland, California
Page 129

Potek, Malcom
Minneapolis, Minnesota
Page 47

Simon, Barbara Becker
Cape Coral, Florida
Pages 24, 37, and 67

Smith, Serena J. A.
The Dalles, Oregon
Page 124

Svetlick, Barbara
Fort Lauderdale, Florida
Page 125

Symons, Jill A.
Peachtree City, Georgia
Pages 25, 66, and 77

Trimlett, Heather
El Cajon, California
Pages 77 and 89

Wolfersberger, Pamela
Lewis Center, Ohio
Page 77

Index